Oxford Introductions to Language Study

Rod Ellis is Professor in the
Department of Applied Language
Studies and Linguistics at the
University of Auckland,
New Zealand.

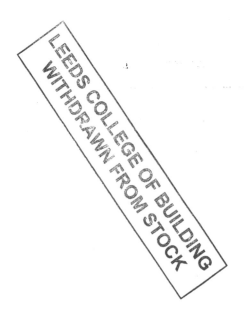

Oxford Introductions to Language Study

Series Editor H.G.Widdowson

Second Language Acquisition

Rod Ellis

OXFORD UNIVERSITY PRESS

Oxford University Press
Great Clarendon Street, Oxford OX2 6DP

Oxford New York
Auckland Bangkok Buenos Aires Cape Town Chennai
Dar es Salaam Delhi Hong Kong Istanbul Karachi Kolkata
Kuala Lumpur Madrid Melbourne Mexico City Mumbai
Nairobi São Paulo Shanghai Taipei Tokyo Toronto

OXFORD and OXFORD ENGLISH
are trade marks of Oxford University Press

ISBN 0 19 437212 X

© Oxford University Press 1997

First published 1997
Eighth impression 2003

Set by Wyvern Typesetting Ltd, Bristol
Printed in Hong Kong

Contents

Preface

Purpose

What justification might there be for a series of introductions to language study? After all, linguistics is already well served with introductory texts: expositions and explanations which are comprehensive and authoritative and excellent in their way. Generally speaking, however, their way is the essentially academic one of providing a detailed initiation into the discipline of linguistics, and they tend to be lengthy and technical: appropriately so, given their purpose. But they can be quite daunting to the novice. There is also a need for a more general and gradual introduction to language: transitional texts which will ease people into an understanding of complex ideas. This series of introductions is designed to serve this need.

Their purpose, therefore, is not to supplant but to support the more academically oriented introductions to linguistics: to prepare the conceptual ground. They are based on the belief that it is an advantage to have a broad map of the terrain sketched out before one considers its more specific features on a smaller scale, a general context in reference to which the detail makes sense. It is sometimes the case that students are introduced to detail without it being made clear what it is a detail *of*. Clearly, a general understanding of ideas is not sufficient: there needs to be closer scrutiny. But equally, close scrutiny can be myopic and meaningless unless it is related to the larger view. Indeed, it can be said that the precondition of more particular enquiry is an awareness of what, in general, the particulars are about. This series is designed to provide this large-scale view of different areas of language study. As such it can serve as a preliminary to (and precondition for) the more specific and specialized enquiry which students of linguistics are required to undertake.

But the series is not only intended to be helpful to such students. There are many people who take an interest in language without being academically engaged in linguistics *per se*. Such people may recognize the importance of understanding language for their own lines of enquiry, or for their own practical purposes, or quite simply for making them aware of something which figures so centrally in their everyday lives. If linguistics has revealing and relevant things to say about language, then this should presumably not be a privileged revelation, but one accessible to people other than linguists. These books have been so designed as to accommodate these broader interests too: they are meant to be introductions to language more generally as well as to linguistics as a discipline.

Design

The books in the series are all cut to the same basic pattern. There are four parts: Survey, Readings, References, and Glossary.

Survey

This is a summary overview of the main features of the area of language study concerned: its scope and principles of enquiry, its basic concerns and key concepts. These are expressed and explained in ways which are intended to make them as accessible as possible to people who have no prior knowledge or expertise in the subject. The Survey is written to be readable and is uncluttered by the customary scholarly references. In this sense, it is simple. But it is not simplistic. Lack of specialist expertise does not imply an inability to understand or evaluate ideas. Ignorance means lack of knowledge, not lack of intelligence. The Survey, therefore, is meant to be challenging. It draws a map of the subject area in such a way as to stimulate thought, and to invite a critical participation in the exploration of ideas. This kind of conceptual cartography has its dangers of course: the selection of what is significant, and the manner of its representation will not be to the liking of everybody, particularly not, perhaps, to some of those inside the discipline. But these surveys are written in the belief that there must be an alternative to a technical account on the one hand and an idiot's guide on the other if linguistics is to be made relevant to people in the wider world.

Readings

Some people will be content to read, and perhaps re-read, the summary Survey. Others will want to pursue the subject and so will use the Survey as the preliminary for more detailed study. The Readings provide the necessary transition. For here the reader is presented with texts extracted from the specialist literature. The purpose of these readings is quite different from the Survey. It is to get readers to focus on the specifics of what is said and how it is said in these source texts. Questions are provided to further this purpose: they are designed to direct attention to points in each text, how they compare across texts, and how they deal with the issues discussed in the survey. The idea is to give readers an initial familiarity with the more specialist idiom of the linguistics literature, where the issues might not be so readily accessible, and to encourage them into close critical reading.

References

One way of moving into more detailed study is through the Readings. Another is through the annotated References in the third section of each book. Here there is a selection of works (books and articles) for further reading. Accompanying comments indicate how these deal in more detail with the issues discussed in the different chapters of the survey.

Glossary

Certain terms in the Survey appear in bold. These are terms used in a special or technical sense in the discipline. Their meanings are made clear in the discussion, but they are also explained in the Glossary at the end of each book. The Glossary is cross-referenced to the Survey, and therefore serves at the same time as an index. This enables readers to locate the term and what it signifies in the more general discussion, thereby, in effect, using the Survey as a summary work of reference.

Use

The series has been designed so as to be flexible in use. Each title is separate and self-contained, with only the basic format in common. The four sections of the format, as described here, can be drawn upon and combined in different ways, as required by the needs, or interests, of different readers. Some may be content with the Survey and the Glossary and may not want to follow up the suggested references. Some may not wish to venture into the Readings. Again, the Survey might be considered as appropriate preliminary reading for a course in applied linguistics or teacher education, and the Readings more appropriate for seminar discussion during the course. In short, the notion of an introduction will mean different things to different people, but in all cases the concern is to provide access to specialist knowledge and stimulate an awareness of its significance. This series as a whole has been designed to provide this access and promote this awareness in respect to different areas of language study.

H.G.WIDDOWSON

Survey

1
Introduction: describing and explaining L2 acquisition

What is 'second language acquisition'?

The systematic study of how people acquire a second language (often referred to as an L2) is a fairly recent phenomenon, belonging to the second half of the twentieth century. Its emergence at this time is perhaps no accident. This has been a time of the 'global village' and the 'World Wide Web', when communication between people has expanded way beyond their local speech communities. As never before, people have had to learn a second language, not just as a pleasing pastime, but often as a means of obtaining an education or securing employment. At such a time, there is an obvious need to discover more about how second languages are learned.

At first sight, the meaning of the term 'second language acquisition' seems transparent but, in fact, it requires careful explanation. For one thing, in this context 'second' can refer to any language that is learned subsequent to the mother tongue. Thus, it can refer to the learning of a third or fourth language. Also, 'second' is not intended to contrast with 'foreign'. Whether you are learning a language naturally as a result of living in a country where it is spoken, or learning it in a classroom through instruction, it is customary to speak generically of 'second' language acquisition.

'L2 acquisition', then, can be defined as the way in which people learn a language other than their mother tongue, inside or outside of a classroom, and 'Second Language Acquisition' (SLA) as the study of this.

What are the goals of SLA?

Imagine that you are an SLA researcher, interested in finding out how learners acquire an L2. How would you set about doing it? One way might be simply to ask learners who have been successful in learning a second language how they did it. This approach has been used and has provided some valuable insights. It is, however, somewhat limited in that learners are probably not aware of or cannot remember the actual learning processes they engaged in. A better approach might be to find out what learners actually do, as opposed to what they think they do, when they try to learn an L2. One way of doing this is by collecting samples of **learner language**—the language that learners produce when they are called on to use an L2 in speech or writing—and analyse them carefully. These samples provide evidence of what the learners know about the language they are trying to learn (the **target language**). If samples are collected at different points in time it may also be possible to find out how learners' knowledge gradually develops. What we might seek to do, then, is to *describe* how learner language changes over time.

But what exactly should you look for in samples of learner language? You may decide to focus on how learners' overall ability to communicate develops, how they become more fluent in their use of an L2. In general, however, SLA has not focused on these communicative aspects of language development but on the formal features of language that linguists have traditionally concentrated on. One example might be the pronunciation of an L2; how learners' accents change over time. Another might be the words learners use; how learners build up their vocabulary. Most often, however, the focus has been the grammar of the L2. Researchers select a specific grammatical structure, such as plurals or relative clauses, and explore how learners' ability to produce this structure develops over time.

One of the goals of SLA, then, is the *description* of L2 acquisition. Another is *explanation*; identifying the external and internal factors that account for why learners acquire an L2 in the way they do.

One of the external factors is the social milieu in which learning takes place. Social conditions influence the opportunities that learners have to hear and speak the language and the attitudes that they develop towards it. For example, it is one thing to learn a language when you respect and are respected by native speakers of that language. It is entirely different when you experience hostility from native speakers or when you wish to distance yourself from them.

Another external factor is the **input** that learners receive, that is, the samples of language to which a learner is exposed. Language learning cannot occur without some input. A question of considerable interest is what type of input facilitates learning. For example, do learners benefit more from input that has been simplified for them or from the authentic language of native-speaker communication?

L2 acquisition can be explained in part by these external factors but we also need to consider internal factors. Learners possess cognitive mechanisms which enable them to extract information about the L2 from the input—to notice, for example, that plurality in English is conveyed by adding an -s to a noun or that the relative pronouns 'who' and 'which' substitute respectively for human and non-human nouns.

L2 learners bring an enormous amount of knowledge to the task of learning an L2. For a start, they have already learned a language (their mother tongue) and we can expect them to draw on this when they learn an L2. They also possess general knowledge about the world which they can draw on to help them understand L2 input. Finally, learners possess communication strategies that can help them make effective use of their L2 knowledge. For example, even if they have not learned the word 'art gallery' they may be able to communicate the idea of it by inventing their own term (for example, 'picture place').

It is also possible that learners are equipped with knowledge of how language in general works and that this helps them to learn a particular language. Let us consider a grammatical example. Learners of L2 English faced with the sentence

Joan wanted Mary to help herself.

may be able to rule out automatically the possibility that the reflexive pronoun 'herself' refers to 'Joan' rather than 'Mary' because they 'know' how such reflexive pronouns work in language in general. According to this view, there are inbuilt constraints on what is grammatically possible in language in general and knowing these makes the task of learning a particular L2 much easier.

A final set of internal factors explain why learners vary in the rate they learn an L2 and how successful they ultimately are. For example, it has been suggested that people vary in their **language aptitude** (i.e. their natural disposition for learning an L2), some finding it easier than others.

The goals of SLA, then, are to describe how L2 acquisition proceeds and to explain this process and why some learners seem to be better at it than others. To illustrate more specifically how SLA researchers have set about trying to achieve these goals we will now examine two case studies of L2 learners.

Two case studies

A **case study** is a detailed study of a learner's acquisition of an L2. It is typically longitudinal, involving the collection of samples of the learner's speech or writing over a period of time, sometimes years. The two case studies which we will now examine were both longitudinal. One is of an adult learner learning English in surroundings where it serves as a means of daily communication and the other of two children learning English in a classroom.

A case study of an adult learner

Wes was a thirty-three year-old artist, a native speaker of Japanese. He had had little formal instruction in English, having left school at fifteen. While he remained in Japan his contacts with native speakers were few and far between. It was only when he began to visit Hawaii, in connection with his work, that he had regular opportunities to use English. Wes, then, is an example of a 'naturalistic' learner—someone who learns the language at the same time as learning to communicate in it.

Richard Schmidt, a researcher at the University of Hawaii, studied Wes's language development over a three-year period from the time he first started visiting Hawaii until he eventually took up residence there. Schmidt asked Wes to make recordings in English when he went on trips back to Tokyo. He then made written transcriptions of these monologues, which lasted between one and three hours. In addition, Schmidt made recordings and transcriptions of informal conversations between Wes and friends in Honolulu.

Among other things, Schmidt was interested in how Wes's knowledge of English grammar developed over the three years. To this end he focused on a small number of grammatical features, such as the use of auxiliary *be*, plural *-s* (for example, 'spoon*s*'), third person *-s* (for example, 'come*s*'), and regular past tense (for example, 'jump*ed*'). He looked to see how accurately Wes used these features in his speech at a time near the beginning of his study and at a time near the end.

What might constitute evidence that Wes was acquiring the grammar of English? Strong evidence would be if Schmidt could show that Wes had learned to use the grammatical features with the same level of accuracy as native speakers of English. In fact, Wes could already use some of the features with native-like accuracy at the beginning of his study. However, Schmidt suspected that Wes had not really acquired these. For example, although Wes did succeed in using progressive *-ing* when it was required, as in:

All day I'm sitt*ing* table.

he also supplied it in sentences when it was not required:

So yesterday I didn't paint*ing*.

Furthermore, there were very few verbs which Wes used in both the simple form (for example, 'paint') and the progressive form (for example, 'painting'). He generally used each verb with just one of these forms. Clearly, Wes did not have the same knowledge of progressive *-ing* as a native speaker.

In fact, Wes had little or no knowledge at the beginning of the study of most of the grammatical structures Schmidt investigated. Moreover, he was still far short of native-speaker accuracy three years later. For example, he continued to omit *-s* from plural nouns, rarely put *-s* on the third person singular of verbs, and never used the regular past tense.

It would be wrong, however, to think of Wes as a complete failure as a language learner. Although he did not learn much grammar, he did develop in other ways. For example, a general feature of Wes's use of English was his use of **formulas**—fixed expressions such as 'Hi! How's it?', 'So, what's new?', 'Whaddya want?', and 'I dunno why'. Schmidt noted that Wes was adept at identifying these fixed phrases and that he practised them consciously. They helped him develop fluency in using English. In fact, Wes achieved considerable success as a communicator. He became quite a skilled conversationalist, very effective at negotiating complex business deals in English and even able to give talks about his paintings in English. He was also highly skilled at repairing communication breakdowns.

A case study of two child learners

Whereas Schmidt studied an adult learner in naturalistic surroundings, I investigated two child learners in a classroom context. Both were almost complete beginners in English at the beginning of the study. J was a ten-year-old Portuguese boy, literate in his native language. He was an adventurous and confident learner, willing to struggle to communicate in English, even when he had very limited resources. R was an eleven-year-old boy from Pakistan, speaking (but unable to write) Punjabi as his native language. Initially, he lacked confidence, using his native language extensively and relying on his elder sister to help him communicate in English. Gradually, however, he became more confident and independent.

Both learners were learning English in a language unit in London. The unit catered exclusively for L2 learners who had recently arrived in Britain. The goal was to prepare students for transfer to local secondary schools. J spent almost four school terms in the unit (about twelve months). R spent two whole school years in the unit and, in fact, was still there when the study ended. The instruction the two learners received was very mixed. It involved both formal language instruction (i.e. attempts to teach the learners specific language items and rules) and more informal instruction (i.e. attempts to get the students to use English communicatively). Initially, at least, the two learners had little exposure to the target language outside the classroom.

The focus of my study was requests. I wanted to find out how the two learners acquired the ability to perform requests for services and goods over the period of study. Requests can be performed in a variety of ways in English, for example:

Give me your pencil.
Can I have your pencil?
Would you mind giving me your pencil?

They can be relatively simple, as in the above examples, or they can be quite complex, as when the speaker offers a reason for making the request:

My pencil's broken. Would you mind giving me yours?

Because English was the medium of communication in these learners' classrooms there were numerous opportunities for them to hear and to perform requests. I collected samples of the two learners' requests by visiting their classrooms regularly and writing down any requests they produced.

When I analysed J's and R's requests, I found clear evidence of development taking place. Moreover, the two learners appeared to develop in much the same way. Initially, their requests were verbless. For example, when J needed a cut out of a big circle in a mathematics lesson he said:

Big circle.

while, in a different lesson, R just pointed at a piece of card to let the teacher know that he wanted him to put a staple in it, saying:

Sir.

A little later, both learners began to use imperative verbs in their requests:

Give me.
Give me a paper.

Some time after this, they learned to use 'Can I have ____?':

Can I have one yellow book, please?

The next stage of their development of requests was marked by a general extension of the linguistic devices they used. For example, R made use of 'want' statements:

Miss, I want. (R wanted the teacher to give him the stapler.)

J used 'got':

You got a rubber?

Occasionally, both learners used hints instead of direct requests. For example, when J wanted the teacher to give him a different coloured piece of paper he said:

This paper is not very good to colour blue.

Finally, the learners began to use 'can' with a range of different verbs (i.e. not just with 'have'):

Can you pass me my pencil?

A number of points emerge from this. One is that both learners were capable of successfully performing simple requests even when they knew very little English. Another is both learners manifested development in their ability to perform requests over the period of study. In particular, they acquired alternative ways of performing them. A third point is that many of their requests seemed formulaic in nature. That is, they used fixed expressions like 'Can I have a ____?' or 'Have you got a ____?' A fourth point is that both learners progressed in much the same way despite the fact that they had different native languages.

By the end of the study, therefore, the two learners' ability to use requests had grown considerably. However, it was equally clear that this ability was limited in a number of respects. Their requests tended to be very direct (i.e. they mostly took the form of commands with an imperative verb) throughout, whereas native speakers would tend to use more indirect requests (for example, they make requests by asking questions or giving hints). The learners' requests were generally very simple. They rarely modified a request and, if they did so, relied more or less exclusively on the one modifier 'please'. Also, whereas native speakers of English vary the way they perform a request with different addressees to ensure politeness, the two learners used the same range of request strategies irrespective of whether they were talking to the teacher or other students. In short, despite ample opportunity to master requests, the two learners were still far short of native-like competence at the end of the study.

What do these case studies show us? First, they raise a number of important methodological issues relating to how L2 acquisition should be studied. Second, they raise issues relating to the description of learner language. Third, they point to some of the problems researchers experience in trying to explain L2 acquisition.

Methodological issues

One issue has to do with what it is that needs to be described. Schmidt was concerned broadly with how Wes developed the ability to communicate in an L2, examining his grammatical development, his ability to use English in situationally appropriate ways, and how he learned to hold successful conversations. My goal was narrower; I was concerned with how J and R acquired the ability to perform a single language function (requests). In this respect, my study is more typical of SLA. Language is such a complex phenomenon that researchers have generally preferred to focus on some specific aspect rather than on the whole of it.

Another issue concerns what it means to say that a learner has 'acquired' a feature of the target language. Schmidt, like many other researchers, defines 'acquisition' in terms of whether the learner manifests patterns of language use that are more or less the same as native speakers of the target language. It might be argued, however, that this conflates what learners *know* with what they *can do*. For example, Wes might be said to know how to make plurals even though he does not always add an -*s* to a plural noun.

There is another problem in determining whether learners have 'acquired' a particular feature. Both Schmidt and I point out that the learners made considerable use of fixed expressions or formulas. Learners may manifest target-like use of a feature in a formula without having acquired the ability to use the feature productively. For example, both J and R acquired the pattern 'Can I have a ___?' early on, but it took them some time to use 'can' in other kinds of sentences. Is it possible to say they had acquired 'can' if they could only use it in one fixed expression? Most researchers would say 'no'.

A third problem in trying to measure whether 'acquisition' has taken place concerns learners' **overuse** of linguistic forms. Schmidt showed that Wes knew when to use the present progressive correctly but he also showed that Wes used this form in contexts that did not require it. In other words, Wes used the form of the present progressive with the wrong function. SLA researchers recognize the need to investigate how the relationship between form and function in learners' output compares with that of native speakers.

Issues in the description of learner language

Both of these studies set out how to describe how learners' use of an L2 changes over time and what this shows about the nature of their knowledge of the L2.

One finding is that learners make **errors** of different kinds. Wes failed to use some grammatical features at all and used others incorrectly. These are errors of omission and overuse. J and R also made grammatical errors in their requests. In addition, they made sociolinguistic errors. That is, they failed to use requests in a socially appropriate manner.

Another finding is that L2 learners acquire a large number of formulaic chunks, which they use to perform communicative functions that are important to them and which contribute to the fluency of their unplanned speech. An important issue in SLA is the role that these formulas play, not just in enhancing learners' performance but also in their acquisition of an L2. Does learning a formula like 'Can I have a ____?' help learners to discover how 'can' works grammatically in the language?

One of the most interesting issues raised by these case studies is whether learners acquire the language systematically. Schmidt found that the order of accuracy of the different grammatical features that he investigated was the same at the beginning of his study as at the end. Thus, at both times, features like progressive -*ing* and auxiliary *be* (for example, He *is* painting) were used accurately while features like past regular and possessive -*s* (for example, 'the woman'*s* dress') were used very inaccurately. I found evidence to suggest that both J and R followed the same sequence of development in their acquisition of requests. These studies, then, suggest that learners do acquire aspects of an L2 systematically and, moreover, that they follow particular developmental routes, with some features being acquired before others. A key question is how universal these developmental patterns are. Do all L2 learners learn following the same route?

Issues in the explanation of L2 acquisition

What can account for these descriptive findings? We can begin with the hypothesis that L2 acquisition involves different kinds of learning. On the one hand, learners internalize chunks of language structure (i.e. formulas). On the other hand, they acquire rules (i.e. the knowledge that a given linguistic feature is used in a particular context with a particular function). In other words, learners must engage in both **item learning** and **system learning**. When learners learn the expression 'Can I have a ____?' they are engaging in item learning—they learn the expression as an unanalysed whole. When they learn that 'can' is followed by a variety of verbs ('have', 'run', 'help', etc.) and that it can express a variety of functions (ability, possibility, permission, etc.) they are engaging in system learning—they are learning some kind of **rule** for 'can'. Learners engage in both types of learning. An explanation of L2 acquisition must account for both item and system learning and how the two interrelate.

The systematic nature of L2 acquisition also requires explanation. Why did Wes seem to learn some grammatical items before others? Why did J and R learn the different ways of making a request in the particular sequence they did? There are a number of possible explanations. One is that learners follow a particular developmental pattern because their mental faculties are structured in such a way that this is the way they *have to* learn. These faculties, it is argued, regulate what learners take from the input and how they store the information in their memories. However, as we will see later, this **mentalist** account of how L2 acquisition takes place is not the only possible one. Other explanations emphasize the importance of external as opposed to internal factors.

None of the three learners in the two case studies reached a native-speaker level of performance. Wes did not learn much grammar. J and R learned a fairly limited range of requests and did not learn how to vary their use of them in accordance with social factors. Why was acquisition in these learners so incomplete? One possibility, of course, is that they simply needed more time to learn. But it is also possible that L2 learners, unlike children acquiring their L1, just stop learning. Perhaps learners like Wes and J and R are only motivated to learn an L2 to the extent that they are able to satisfy their communicative needs. After all, it is not necessary to learn the full grammar of a language in order to get one's meanings across. There are other explanations, however. Perhaps all three learners did not wish to belong to the community of native speakers they had contact with and, therefore, kept a linguistic 'distance' between themselves and them. Perhaps it is only possible to acquire native-speaker competence if learners start very young when their brains are, in some sense, open to language. Perhaps L2 learners can only acquire difficult linguistic features if they receive direct instruction in them.

These case studies, then, illuminate the kinds of issues that pre-occupy SLA. These issues will figure in subsequent chapters.

2
The nature of learner language

We have seen that the main way of investigating L2 acquisition is by collecting and describing samples of learner language. The description may focus on the kinds of errors learners make and how these errors change over time, or it may identify developmental patterns by describing the stages in the acquisition of particular grammatical features such as past tense, or it may examine the variability found in learner language. Let us consider each of these three areas in turn.

Errors and error analysis

At first sight, it may seem rather odd to focus on what learners get wrong rather than on what they get right. However, there are good reasons for focusing on errors. First, they are a conspicuous feature of learner language, raising the important question of 'Why do learners make errors?' Second, it is useful for teachers to know what errors learners make. Third, paradoxically, it is possible that making errors may actually help learners to learn when they self-correct the errors they make.

Identifying errors

The first step in analysing learner errors is to identify them. This is in fact easier said than done. Look at the sample of learner language below. This is a transcription of a story, based on a series of pictures, told by Jean, an adult French learner of English. He told the story orally after having been given the chance to write it out first. Can you identify all the errors?

One day an Indian gentleman, a snake charmer, arrived in England by plane. He was coming from Bombay with two pieces of luggage. The big of them contained a snake. A man and a little boy was watching him in the customs area. The man said to the little boy 'Go and speak with this gentleman.' When the little boy was speaking with the traveller, the thief took the big suitcase and went out quickly. When the victim saw that he cried 'Help me! Help me! A thief A thief!' The policeman was in this corner whistle but it was too late. The two thieves escape with the big suitcase, took their car and went in the traffic. They passed near a zoo and stop in a forest. There they had a big surprise. The basket contain a big snake.

To identify errors we have to compare the sentences learners produce with what seem to be the normal or 'correct' sentences in the target language which correspond with them. Sometimes this is fairly straightforward. For example, Jean says:

A man and a little boy *was* watching him.

It is not difficult to see that the correct sentence should be:

A man and a little boy *were* watching him.

By comparing the two sentences we can see that Jean has used 'was' instead of 'were'—an error in subject–verb agreement. Sometimes, however, learners produce sentences that are possible target-language sentences but not preferred ones. For example, Jean says:

… went *in* the traffic.

Is this an error? A native speaker would probably prefer to say:

… went *into* the traffic.

but '*in* the traffic' is not actually ungrammatical.

At other times, it is difficult to reconstruct the correct sentence because we are not sure what the learner meant to say. An example is when Jean says:

The *big* of them contained a snake.

One way of reconstructing the correct sentence is:

The *bigger* of them contained a snake.

According to this reconstruction, Jean has used 'big' instead of 'bigger'—an error in the use of a comparative adjective. But another possible way of reconstructing the sentence is:

The big *one* contained a snake.

Here the error lies in using 'big of them' instead of 'big one'—an error in the use of the pronoun 'one'. It is clear that identifying the exact errors that learners make is often difficult.

There is a further problem. How can be we be sure that when a learner produces a deviant form it is not just an accidental slip of the tongue? After all, native speakers often make slips when they are tired or under some kind of pressure to communicate. We need to distinguish **errors** and **mistakes**. Errors reflect gaps in a learner's knowledge; they occur because the learner does not know what is correct. Mistakes reflect occasional lapses in performance; they occur because, in a particular instance, the learner is unable to perform what he or she knows.

There is an example of an apparent 'mistake' in Jean's speech. Early in the narrative he says:

The big of them *contained* a snake.

using the past tense of the verb 'contain' correctly. However, in the final sentence he says:

The basket *contain* a snake.

making what seems to be a past tense error. But clearly Jean *knows* what the past tense of 'contain' is as he has already used it correctly once. His failure to say 'contained' in the last sentence, then, might be considered a mistake.

How can we distinguish errors and mistakes? One way might be to check the consistency of learners' performance. If they consistently substitute 'contain' for 'contained' this would indicate a lack of knowledge—an error. However, if they sometimes say 'contain' and sometimes 'contained', this would suggest that they possess knowledge of the correct form and are just slipping up—a mistake. Another way might be to ask learners to try to correct their own deviant utterances. Where they are unable to, the deviations are errors; where they are successful, they are mistakes. However, as we will see later, when we examine variability in learner language, it is not as simple as this. Learners may consistently use a feature like past tense in some contexts and consistently fail to use it in others. Ultimately, a clear distinction between an error and a mistake may not be possible.

Describing errors

Once all the errors have been identified, they can be described and classified into types. There are several ways of doing this. One way is to classify errors into grammatical categories. We could gather all the errors relating to verbs and then identify the different kinds of verb errors in our sample—errors in the past tense, for example. Another way might be to try to identify general ways in which the learners' utterances differ from the reconstructed target-language utterances. Such ways include 'omission' (i.e. leaving out an item that is required for an utterance to be considered grammatical), 'misinformation' (i.e. using one grammatical form in place of another grammatical form), and 'misordering' (i.e. putting the words in an utterance in the wrong order). Classifying errors in these ways can help us to diagnose learners' learning problems at any one stage of their development and, also, to plot how changes in error patterns occur over time.

An analysis of Jean's errors reveals that the most common grammatical category of error is 'past tense'; Jean fails to use the past tense on a number of occasions. The most common general error type is 'misinformation' (for example, the use of 'big' instead of 'bigger', of 'was watching' instead of 'were watching' and, perhaps, of 'in the traffic' instead of 'into the traffic'). All the past tense errors are also misinformation errors.

Explaining errors

The identification and description of errors are preliminaries to the much more interesting task of trying to explain why they occur. Errors are, to a large extent, systematic and, to a certain extent, predictable. Thus, Jean's verb errors described above do not involve haphazard substitutions of past tense verbs. We do not find him using the present progressive form (for example, 'containing') in place of the past tense form on some occasions and the simple form (for example, 'contain') on others. Instead, we find evidence of regular replacements using a single form. All of Jean's past tense errors involve the use of the simple form of the verb. This systematicity suggests that Jean has constructed some kind of **rule**, albeit a rule different from that of the target language.

Errors are not only systematic; many of them are also universal. Thus, the kind of past tense error found in Jean's speech has been attested in the speech of many learners. In fact, most, if not all learners go through a stage of learning where they substitute the simple form of the verb for the past tense form.

Of course, not all errors are universal. Some errors are common only to learners who share the same mother tongue or whose mother tongues manifest the same linguistic property. For example, speakers of Bantu languages in southern Africa frequently use the preposition 'at' to refer to direction as well as location, producing errors such as:

We went *at* Johannesburg last weekend.

This error appears to be explained by the fact that Bantu languages employ a single preposition to express location and direction where English has two (i.e. 'at' and 'to').

Errors, then, can have different sources. Some errors seem to be universal, reflecting learners' attempts to make the task of learning and using the L2 simpler. Learners commit errors of **omission**. For example, they leave out the articles 'a' and 'the' and leave the -*s* off plural nouns. They also overgeneralize forms that they find easy to learn and process. The use of 'eated' in place of 'ate' is an example of an **overgeneralization** error. Both errors of omission and overgeneralization are common in the speech of all L2 learners, irrespective of their L1. Other errors, however, reflect learners' attempts to make use of their L1 knowledge. These are known as **transfer** errors. Irrespective of the type of error, however, learners are to be seen as actively involved in shaping the 'grammars' they are learning. Learners 'create' their own rules.

Error evaluation

Where the purpose of the error analysis is to help learners learn an L2, there is a need to evaluate errors. Some errors can be considered more serious than others because they are more likely to interfere with the intelligibility of what someone says. Teachers will want to focus their attention on these.

Some errors, known as **global errors,** violate the overall structure of a sentence and for this reason may make it difficult to process. Jean, for example, says:

The policeman was in this corner whistle ...

which is difficult to understand because the basic structure of the sentence is wrong. Other errors, known as **local errors,** affect only a single constituent in the sentence (for example, the verb) and are, perhaps, less likely to create any processing problems. Most of Jean's errors are of this kind. This may be why his oral narrative is quite easy to follow despite all the errors.

Developmental patterns

We have seen that many of the errors that L2 learners make are universal: all learners, no matter whether they are learning naturalistically or in a classroom, and irrespective of their L1, make omission, overgeneralization, and transfer errors. We can also explore the universality of L2 acquisition by examining the developmental pattern learners follow.

The early stages of L2 acquisition

We can find out how a language is learned as a natural, untutored process by investigating what learners do when exposed to the L2 in communicative settings.

In such circumstances, some L2 learners, particularly if they are children, undergo a **silent period**. That is, they make no attempt to say anything to begin with. Of course, they may be learning a lot about the language just through listening to or reading it. The silent period may serve as a preparation for subsequent production. Some learners talk to themselves in the L2 even when they decline to talk to other people.

When learners do begin to speak in the L2 their speech is likely to manifest two particular characteristics. One is the kind of formulaic chunks which we saw in the case studies. Fixed expressions like 'How do you do?', 'I don't know', 'Can I have a ___?', 'My name is ___' figure very prominently in early L2 learning. They provide learners with the means of performing useful language functions such as greetings and requests. These ready-made chunks of language can give a mistaken impression of competence.

The second characteristic of early L2 speech is propositional simplification. Learners find it difficult to speak in full sentences so they frequently leave words out. For example, J wanted the teacher to give him a blue crayon but said only:

Me no blue.

meaning 'I don't have a blue crayon'. Interestingly this reduced speech is very similar to the kind of speech children produce in the early stages of learning their mother tongue. The occurrence of this kind of basic language appears to be a universal of both first and second language acquisition.

In time, though, learners do begin to learn the grammar of the L2. This raises other questions. One concerns the **acquisition order**. Do learners acquire the grammatical structures of an L2 in a definite order? For example, do they learn a feature like progressive -*ing* (as in 'paint*ing*') before a feature like past tense -*ed* (as in paint*ed*). We have already seen that learners do seem to find some grammatical features easier than others, so it is quite possible that acquisition follows a definite order. Another question concerns the **sequence of acquisition** of particular grammatical structures, such as past tense. Do learners learn such structures in a single step or do they proceed through a number of interim stages before they master the target structure?

The order of acquisition

To investigate the order of acquisition, researchers choose a number of grammatical structures to study (for example, progressive -*ing*, auxiliary *be*, and plural -*s*). They then collect samples of learner language and identify how accurately each feature is used by different learners. This enables them to arrive at an **accuracy order**. That is, they rank the features according to how accurately each feature is used by the learners. Some researchers then argue that the accuracy order must be the same as the order of acquisition on the grounds that the more accurately learners are able to use a particular feature the more likely they are to have acquired that feature early.

Researchers have shown that there is a definite accuracy order and that this remains more or less the same irrespective of the learners' mother tongues, their age, and whether or not they have received formal language instruction. Most of the learners they have studied perform progressive *-ing*, auxiliary *be*, and plural *-s* most accurately, suggesting that they acquired these features first. Articles and irregular past come next. The most difficult structures are regular past and third person *-s*. On the basis of these findings, it has been suggested that there must be a natural order of acquisition that all learners follow.

This claim is an important one. It raises crucial theoretical questions as to whether L2 acquisition is the result of environmental factors that govern the input to which learners are exposed, or of internal mental factors which somehow dictate how learners acquire grammatical structures.

We should note here, however, that not all researchers are convinced there is a universal 'natural order'. They have criticized the research on a number of grounds. Some have pointed out, for example, that it may be wrong to assume that the order of accuracy is the same as the order of acquisition. They have produced evidence to show that sometimes learners begin using a structure accurately early on only to start making errors with it later. It cannot be concluded, they have argued, that learners have acquired a structure simply because they can use it accurately, a point considered more fully below. Other researchers have shown that the order does vary somewhat according to the learner's first language. For example, Schmidt found that Wes, whose first language was Japanese, performed plural *-s* very poorly, much less accurately than irregular past. In other words, Wes did not follow the 'natural' order.

Another problem is that the research treats acquisition as if it is a process of accumulating linguistic structures. Acquisition is seen as analogous to building a wall, with one brick set in place before another is placed on top. Such a view is, in fact, seriously mistaken, as studies of individual grammatical structures have made clear. Even the simplest structure is subject to a process of gradual development, manifesting clear stages. To investigate this we need to consider the sequence of acquisition.

Sequence of acquisition

When learners acquire a grammatical structure they do so gradually, moving through a series of stages *en route* to acquiring the native-speaker rule. The acquisition of a particular grammatical structure, therefore, must be seen as a *process* involving **transitional constructions**. As an example of this process, let us consider how L2 learners acquire irregular past tense forms (for example, 'ate'). Learners are likely to pass through the different stages shown in Table 2.1.

Stage	Description	Example
1	Learners fail to mark the verb for past time.	'eat'
2	Learners begin to produce irregular past tense forms.	'ate'
3	Learners overgeneralize the regular past tense form.	'eated'
4	Sometimes learners produce hybrid forms.	'ated'
5	Learners produce correct irregular past tense forms.	'ate'

TABLE 2.1 *Stages in the acquisition of the past tense of 'eat'*

Such sequences are instructive because they reveal that the use of a correct structural form (for example, 'ate') does not necessarily mean that this form has been 'acquired'. Indeed, in this sequence, learners producing 'eated' and 'ated' are, in fact, more advanced than learners at stage 2 who produce 'ate'. Acquisition follows a **U-shaped course of development**; that is, initially learners may display a high level of accuracy only to apparently regress later before finally once again performing in accordance with target-language norms. It is clear that this occurs because learners reorganize their existing knowledge in order to accommodate new knowledge. Thus, stages 2 and 3 only arise when learners have begun to acquire regular -*ed* (as in 'jump*ed*'). Forms like 'eated' and 'ated' represent an overgeneralization of the regular -*ed* past tense. This kind of reorganization, which is believed to be prevalent in L2 acquisition, is referred to as **restructuring**. As learners restructure their grammatical systems, they may appear to regress whereas in fact they are advancing. Sequences such as that for irregular past reveal how restructuring occurs and how it can lead to U-shaped development.

It is clear that the acquisition of what looks like a simple grammatical feature such as past tense is, in fact, a highly complex affair. Not only are there general stages in the acquisition of grammatical features like past tense, as illustrated in Table 2.1, but there may also be stages within stages. Thus, when learners begin to use past tense markers (either irregular markers as in 'ate' or regular markers as in 'painted'), they do not do so on all verbs at the same time. Learners find it easier to mark verbs for past tense if the verb refers to events (for example, 'arrive'), somewhat more difficult to mark verbs that refer to activities (for example, 'sleep'), and most difficult to mark verbs that refer to states (for example, 'want').

The kind of verb also influences the kind of errors learners make. For example, with activity verbs learners are more likely to substitute a progressive form for the past tense form:

After that the weather was nice so we *swimming* in the ocean.

In contrast, with state verbs they substitute the simple form of the verb:

Last night everything *seem* very quiet and peaceful.

Learners, then, pass through highly complex stages of development. These stages are not sharply defined, however. Rather they are blurred as learners oscillate between stages. Thus, in the case of past tense, at any one time a learner may mark some verbs correctly for past tense, fail to mark others at all, and overgeneralize the regular *-ed* and the progressive *-ing* forms with yet other verbs. Despite the complexity of learners' behaviour, however, it is clear that it is far from random.

Some implications

The discovery of common patterns in the way in which learner language changes over time is one of the most important findings of SLA. It provides further support for the conclusions reached from the study of learner errors, namely that L2 acquisition is systematic and, to a large extent, universal, reflecting ways in which internal cognitive mechanisms control acquisition, irrespective of the personal background of learners or the setting in which they learn.

The work on developmental patterns is important for another reason. It suggests that some linguistic features (particularly grammatical ones) are inherently easier to learn than others. For example, the fact that learners master plural -s before third person -s suggests that plural -s is in some sense easier to learn. This has implications for both SLA theory and for language teaching.

Of course, it does not follow that because learners *naturally* learn one feature before another they must *necessarily* do so. A key question for both SLA and language teaching, then, is whether the orders and sequences of acquisition can be altered through formal instruction. We will examine attempts to investigate this in a later section.

Variability in learner language

We have seen that learner language is systematic. That is, at a particular stage of development, learners consistently use the same grammatical form, although this is often different from that employed by native speakers. We have also seen that learner language is variable. At any given stage of development, learners sometimes employ one form and sometimes another. Thus, one type of error may alternate with another type:

Yesterday the thief *steal* the suitcase.
Yesterday the thief *stealing* the suitcase.

or an error may alternate with the correct target-language form:

Yesterday the thief *steal* the suitcase.
Yesterday the thief *stole* the suitcase.

Such was the case with Jean, whose oral narrative (see page 16) displays the use of both correct past tense forms (for example, 'arrived' and 'cried') and erroneous forms (for example, 'whistle' and 'escape'). As we have already noted, there is even one verb ('contain') that occurs in both correct and erroneous forms at different points of the narrative.

These observations do not invalidate the claim that learner

language is systematic since it is possible that variability is also systematic. That is, we may be able to explain, and even predict, when learners use one form and when another.

Indeed, we have already seen evidence of systematic variability. Learners' choice of past tense marker (i.e. zero, progressive form, or correct past tense form) depends, in part, on whether the verb refers to an event, an activity, or a state. Thus, it appears that learners vary in their use of the L2 according to **linguistic context**. In one context they use one form while in other contexts they use alternate forms. In the above example, the linguistic context for the choice of past tense marker is created by the verb itself. In other examples, the crucial element in the linguistic context involves some other constituent of the utterance. For example, learners may behave differently depending on whether or not an adverb of frequency (for example, 'every day' or 'usually') occurs with an activity verb like 'play'. In sentences referring to past time which do not have an adverb of frequency, they are likely to use a progressive marker:

George *playing* football. (= George played football all the time.)

However, in sentences with such an adverb, they are more likely to use the base form of the verb:

In Peru, George usually *play* football every day. (= In Peru, George usually played football every day.)

We can see, then, that one linguistic form can trigger the use of another form.

The effects of linguistic context are also evident in learners' use of the verb 'to be'. Learners sometimes use full 'be' (for example, 'is'), sometimes contracted 'be' (for example, ' 's'), and sometimes omit 'be' entirely. The use of these three forms is determined to a considerable extent by the linguistic context. In one study it was found that the target-language variants (for example, 'is' and ' 's') were used more consistently with pronoun subjects, while 'be' was more likely to be omitted with noun subjects (for example, 'Teacher not here').

Learners also vary the linguistic forms they use in accordance with the **situational context**. In this respect, learners are no different from native speakers. When native speakers of English are talking to friends, for example, they tend to speak informally, using colloquial expressions:

My kid's a real pain these days.

In contrast, when they are talking to someone they do not know very well they tend to use more formal language:

My daughter can be very troublesome these days.

Learners vary their use of language similarly. They are more likely to use the correct target-language forms in formal contexts and non-target forms in informal contexts.

Another important factor that accounts for the systematic nature of variability is the **psycholinguistic context**—whether learners have the opportunity to plan their production. To illustrate how this works we can turn again to Jean. The transcript on page 16 is of the oral narrative that Jean produced after he had been given the chance to write it out. The transcript below is of another oral narrative which Jean produced, this time with no prior opportunity to plan. A comparison of how Jean marks verbs requiring past tense in the two narratives is revealing. First, it is clear that overall Jean uses a higher proportion of irregular verbs like 'saw' and 'went' in the unplanned narrative than in the planned one. Second, Jean is much more likely to mark verbs correctly for past tense in the planned than in the unplanned narrative. This is true for both regular and irregular verbs but especially so for the latter. In fact, in the unplanned narrative he fails to mark a single regular verb for past tense. It is clear that Jean's use of the past tense is strongly influenced by the availability of planning time. He is more likely to use target-language forms when he has time to plan.

One evening a little boy was going at home after the classroom after the class. He went out of the bus with three packets. One of them the small one falled on the ground. He don't saw it but the man who was passing by this way saw it and he would given this packet to the little boy also he took the same way. It was dark but the moon was full. When the little boy saw the man who follow him he was afraid. He run quickly followed by the man. Just before that little boy arrive in his home the man join him and gave him his packet. Then the little boy was happy to receive his packet.

Learners, then, manifest considerable variability in their production of an L2. A question of some interest is whether this variability is simply a matter of performance or whether it reflects the underlying system they are trying to construct. One view is that learners do build variable systems by trying to map particular forms on to particular functions.

A characteristic of any natural language is that forms realize meanings in a systematic way. Learner language is no different. However, the particular **form–function mappings** which learners make do not always conform to those found in the target language. J, one of the learners discussed earlier (see page 8), possessed two forms for expressing negatives at one stage in his development, as shown in these two utterances:

Mariana no coming today.
Don't sit in that one chair.

The two forms are '*no* + verb' and '*don't* + verb'. Earlier J seemed to use these two forms randomly, but at this stage he displayed a measure of consistency. '*No* + verb' was used to make negative statements while '*don't* + verb' was used in negative requests. Learners, it seems, try to make their available linguistic resources work to maximum effect by mapping one meaning on to one form. The resulting systems are often very different from the target-language system. With time, of course, they become more target-like.

Variability in learner language, then, is clearly not just random. Learners have access to two or more linguistic forms for realizing a single grammatical structure but they do not employ these arbitrarily. Rather their choice is determined by a variety of factors such as linguistic context, the situational context, and the availability of planning time. According to one view, this systematicity reflects a variable system of form–function mappings. The question arises as to whether all variability in learner language is systematic or whether some is indeed random. On this point there have been differences of opinion.

It would seem that at least some variability is 'free'. Learners do sometimes use two or more forms in **free variation**. For example,

J produced these two negative utterances in close proximity to each other, in the same context, while addressing the same person and with similar amounts of planning time:

No look my card.
Don't look my card.

Later on, as we have seen, J went on the use these two negative forms systematically.

It is possible that free variation constitutes an essential stage in the acquisition of grammatical structures. Different kinds of variability may be evident at different stages of development. Initially, we might propose, learners begin by acquiring a single form (for example, the simple form of the verb 'paint') and use it for a variety of functions (for example, to refer to future, present, and past time). Later, they acquire other verb forms but initially they use these interchangeably with the simple form. For example, when learners first acquire the past tense form of a verb (for example, 'paint*ed*') they are likely to use this in free variation with the simple form of the verb. Fairly rapidly, they then start to use the forms systematically, for example, using 'painted' in planned discourse and 'paint' in unplanned discourse. Finally, they eliminate non-target forms and use the target-language form to perform the same function as native speakers, using 'painted' consistently to refer to past time.

It is important to recognize that this general sequence of acquisition applies to *specific* grammatical features. Thus, it is possible for individual learners to be at different stages in the sequence for different grammatical features. For example, a learner may be at the completion stage for past tense but at the free variation stage for the articles *a* and *the*.

Not all learners reach the completion stage for every grammatical structure. Many will continue to show non-target language variability in at least some grammatical features. It is for this reason that we can talk of **fossilization**; many learners stop developing while still short of target-language competence. Also, learners may succeed in reaching target-language norms in some types of language use (for example, planned discourse) but not in others (for example, unplanned discourse).

Summary

In this section, we have examined a number of properties of learner language and, in so doing, traced the way in which SLA has evolved as a field of enquiry. Early on, researchers focused on learners' errors, developing procedures for identifying, describing, explaining, and evaluating them. These studies revealed that learners' errors are systematic and that they reflect the stage of development that a learner has reached. An important finding was that learners seem to go beyond the available input, producing errors that show they actively construct rules, which although non-target-like, guide their performance in the L2.

Subsequently, researchers focused on exploring the regularities of L2 acquisition by searching for 'orders' and 'sequences' of acquisition. They found evidence to suggest that learners regularly master some grammatical features before others. However, they soon recognized that treating L2 acquisition as if it involved an accumulation of grammatical features misrepresented what actually occurred. Increasingly, descriptive research in SLA has focused on how learners acquire specific grammatical subsystems such as negatives, interrogatives, relative clauses, and verb tenses like the past tense. It has been able to show that grammatical features manifest clear developmental sequences, involving stages that reflect unique 'rules' not evident in the input to which learners are exposed. Learners seem to be actively involved in shaping how they acquire an L2.

Research on variability has sought to show that, although allowance should perhaps be made for some free variation, variability in learner language is systematic. That is, learners use their linguistic sources in predictable ways. The use of specific grammatical forms has been shown to vary according to the linguistic context, the situational context (for example, who the learner is addressing), and the psycholinguistic context (for example, whether the learner has an opportunity to plan). Furthermore, variability plays an integrative part in the overall pattern of development, with learners moving through a series of stages that reflect different kinds of variability.

In the next chapters we will try to account for these properties of learner language, beginning with the concept of interlanguage.

3

Interlanguage

Earlier we noted that some researchers consider that the systematic development of learner language reflects a mental system of L2 knowledge. This system is often referred to as **interlanguage**. The concept of interlanguage constitutes one of the first attempts to explain L2 acquisition by answering questions such as 'What is the nature of the linguistic representations of the L2 that learners form?' and 'How do these representations change over time?' To understand what is meant by interlanguage we need to briefly consider **behaviourist learning theory** and **mentalist** views of language learning.

Behaviourist learning theory

The dominant psychological theory of the 1950s and 1960s was behaviourist learning theory. According to this theory, language learning is like any other kind of learning in that it involves habit formation. Habits are formed when learners respond to stimuli in the environment and subsequently have their responses reinforced so that they are remembered. Thus, a habit is a stimulus–response connection.

It was believed that all behaviour, including the kind of complex behaviour found in language acquisition, could be explained in terms of habits. Learning took place when learners had the opportunity to practise making the correct response to a given stimulus. Learners imitated models of correct language (i.e. stimuli) and received positive reinforcement if they were correct and negative reinforcement if they were incorrect. For example, learners might hear the sentence 'Give me a pencil', use it themselves, and thereby be rewarded by achieving their communicative goal (i.e. by being given a pencil when they wanted one). It should be clear that behaviourist accounts of L2 acquisition emphasize only what can be directly observed (i.e. the 'input' to the learner and the learner's own 'output') and ignore what goes on in the 'black box' of the learner's mind.

Behaviourism cannot adequately account for L2 acquisition. This is readily apparent from the descriptive work on learner language discussed in the previous chapter. Learners frequently do not produce output that simply reproduces the input. Furthermore, the systematic nature of their errors demonstrates that they are actively involved in constructing their own 'rules', rules that sometimes bear little resemblance to the patterns of language modelled in the input. In short, learning is not just a response to external stimuli.

A mentalist theory of language learning

The obvious inadequacies of behaviourist explanations of L2 acquisition led researchers to look towards an alternative theoretical framework. They did not have to look very far as the 1960s witnessed a major shift in thinking in psychology and linguistics. From a preoccupation with the role of 'nurture' (i.e. how environmental factors shape learning), researchers switched their attention to 'nature' (i.e. how the innate properties of the human mind shape learning). This new paradigm was, therefore, mentalist (or 'nativist') in orientation.

In the 1960s and 1970s a mentalist theory of first language (L1) acquisition emerged. According to this theory:

1 Only human beings are capable of learning language.
2 The human mind is equipped with a faculty for learning language, referred to as a **Language Acquisition Device**. This is separate from the faculties responsible for other kinds of cognitive activity (for example, logical reasoning).
3 This faculty is the primary determinant of language acquisition.
4 Input is needed, but only to 'trigger' the operation of the language acquisition device.

The concept of interlanguage drew directly on these mentalist views of L1 acquisition.

What is 'interlanguage'?

The term 'interlanguage' was coined by the American linguist, Larry Selinker, in recognition of the fact that L2 learners construct a linguistic system that draws, in part, on the learner's L1 but is also different from it and also from the target language. A learner's interlanguage is, therefore, a unique linguistic system.

The concept of interlanguage involves the following premises about L2 acquisition:

1 The learner constructs a system of abstract linguistic rules which underlies comprehension and production of the L2. This system of rules is viewed as a 'mental grammar' and is referred to as an 'interlanguage'.

2 The learner's grammar is permeable. That is, the grammar is open to influence from the outside (i.e. through the input). It is also influenced from the inside. For example, the omission, overgeneralization, and transfer errors which we considered in the previous chapter constitute evidence of internal processing.

3 The learner's grammar is transitional. Learners change their grammar from one time to another by adding rules, deleting rules, and restructuring the whole system. This results in an **interlanguage continuum**. That is, learners construct a series of mental grammars or interlanguages as they gradually increase the complexity of their L2 knowledge. For example, initially learners may begin with a very simple grammar where only one form of the verb is represented (for example, 'paint'), but over time they add other forms (for example, 'painting' and 'painted'), gradually sorting out the functions that these verbs can be used to perform. The transitional nature of interlanguage is also reflected in the sequences of acquisition considered in Chapter 2.

4 Some researchers have claimed that the systems learners construct contain variable rules. That is, they argue that learners

are likely to have competing rules at any one stage of development. However, other researchers argue that interlanguage systems are homogeneous and that variability reflects the mistakes learners make when they try to use their knowledge to communicate. These researchers see variability as an aspect of performance rather than competence. The premise that interlanguage systems are themselves variable is, therefore, a disputed one.

5 Learners employ various **learning strategies** to develop their interlanguages. The different kinds of errors learners produce reflect different learning strategies. For example, omission errors suggest that learners are in some way simplifying the learning task by ignoring grammatical features that they are not yet ready to process. Overgeneralization and transfer errors can also be seen as evidence of learning strategies.

6 The learner's grammar is likely to fossilize. Selinker suggested that only about five per cent of learners go on to develop the same mental grammar as native speakers. The majority stop some way short. The prevalence of **backsliding** (i.e. the production of errors representing an early stage of development) is typical of fossilized learners. Fossilization does not occur in L1 acquisition and thus is unique to L2 grammars.

This concept of interlanguage offers a general account of how L2 acquisition takes place. It incorporates elements from mentalist theories of linguistics (for example, the notion of a 'language acquisition device') and elements from cognitive psychology (for example, 'learning strategies'). It is also somewhat indeterminate in that it does not offer a very precise explanation of what takes place. In fact it is, perhaps, more useful for the questions it raises than the answers it provides. When does input work for acquisition and when does it not? Why do learners sometimes employ an L1 transfer strategy and sometimes an overgeneralization strategy? What makes learner language so variable? What causes learners to restructure their interlanguages? Why does this restructuring result in clearly identifiable sequences of acquisition? Why do most learners fossilize? Clearly, the concept of interlanguage needs to be elaborated to address such questions. The various theories that we shall shortly consider seek to do this.

A computational model of L2 acquisition

The concept of interlanguage can be viewed as a metaphor of how L2 acquisition takes place. It implies that the human mind functions like a computer. Figure 3.1 represents the basic computational metaphor that has grown out of 'interlanguage' and that informs much of SLA. The learner is exposed to input, which is processed in two stages. First, parts of it are attended to and taken into short-term memory. These are referred to as **intake**. Second, some of the intake is stored in long-term memory as L2 knowledge. The processes responsible for creating intake and L2 knowledge occur within the 'black box' of the learner's mind where the learner's interlanguage is constructed. Finally, L2 knowledge is used by the learner to produce spoken and written output (i.e. what we have called learner language).

FIGURE 3.1 *A computational model of L2 acquisition*

As we shall shortly see, this basic model of L2 acquisition can be elaborated in a number of ways. For example, a component labelled 'social context' might be added to explain how the nature of the input varies from one setting to another. The 'L2 knowledge' component can be broken up into two or more components to reflect the different kinds of knowledge learners construct (for example, explicit knowledge *about* language and implicit knowledge *of* language). An arrow can be drawn from 'output' to 'input' to show that what a learner says or writes can also serve as samples of language from which intake can be derived.

We will now explore this computational model by examining a number of perspectives derived from different components of the model. In the process of doing so, we will also introduce a number of other metaphors that seek to provide an explanation of L2 acquisition.

4
Social aspects of interlanguage

The prevailing perspective on interlanguage is psycholinguistic, as reflected in the metaphor of the computer. That is, researchers have been primarily concerned with identifying the internal mechanisms that are responsible for interlanguage development. However, right from the beginning, SLA has also acknowledged the importance of social factors.

Three rather different approaches to incorporating a social angle on the study of L2 acquisition can be identified. The first views interlanguage as consisting of different 'styles' which learners call upon under different conditions of language use. The second concerns how social factors determine the input that learners use to construct their interlanguage. The third considers how the social identities that learners negotiate in their interactions with native speakers shape their opportunities to speak and, thereby, to learn an L2.

Interlanguage as a stylistic continuum

Drawing on work on variability in learner language, Elaine Tarone has proposed that interlanguage involves a **stylistic continuum**. She argues that learners develop a capability for using the L2 and that this underlies '*all* regular language behavior'. This capability, which constitutes 'an abstract linguistic system', is comprised of a number of different 'styles' which learners access in accordance with a variety of factors. At one end of the continuum is the **careful style**, evident when learners are consciously attending to their choice of linguistic forms, as when they feel the need to be 'correct'. At the other end of the continuum is the

vernacular style, evident when learners are making spontaneous choices of linguistic form, as is likely in free conversation.

An example will help to make Tarone's model clear. Japanese learners find it difficult to learn the sound /z/, as in 'zoo' and 'churches'. Now, imagine that we collect samples of spoken English from a number of Japanese learners over a period of time and under different conditions of language use—free speech, reading a dialogue, and reading lists of isolated words. What would we find? One study found Japanese learners produced /z/ most accurately when reading isolated words and least accurately in free speech. They produced it at a level between these two when reading a dialogue. This study also showed that over time the learners improved their ability to use /z/ accurately in their careful style (i.e. when reading lists of words) to a much greater extent than in their vernacular style (i.e. in free speech).

Tarone's idea of interlanguage as a stylistic continuum is attractive in a number of ways. It explains why learner language is variable. It suggests that an interlanguage grammar, although different from a native speaker's grammar, is constructed according to the same principles, for native speakers have been shown to possess a similar range of styles. It relates language use to language learning. However, as Tarone herself has acknowledged, the model also has a number of problems. First, later research has shown that learners are not always most accurate in their careful style and least accurate in their vernacular style. Sometimes L2 speakers show greatest accuracy in the vernacular style, for example, when a specific grammatical feature is of special importance for conveying a particular meaning in conversation.

A second problem is that the role of social factors remains unclear. Native speakers style-shift in accordance with whom they are addressing, using a careful style with non-familiar addressees, especially if they are socially subordinate to them, and a vernacular style with familiar addressees who are their social equals. In other words, style-shifting among native speakers reflects the social group they belong to. This is not necessarily the case for L2 learners, however. It is doubtful, for example, whether the concept of 'social group' is applicable to classroom learners of foreign languages. Yet such learners 'style-shift', as the study of the Japanese learners referred to above demonstrates.

This suggests that the variability evident in their language use is psycholinguistically rather than socially motivated (i.e. it reflects opportunities to plan output). In short, Tarone's theory seems to relate more to psycholinguistic rather than social factors in variation.

Another theory that also draws on the idea of stylistic variation but which is more obviously social is Howard Giles's **accommodation theory**. This seeks to explain how a learner's social group influences the course of L2 acquisition. For Giles the key idea is that of 'social accommodation'. He suggests that when people interact with each other they either try to make their speech similar to that of their addressee in order to emphasize social cohesiveness (a process of **convergence**) or to make it different in order to emphasize their social distinctiveness (a process of **divergence**). It has been suggested that L2 acquisition involves 'long-term convergence'. That is, when the social conditions are such that learners are motivated to converge on native-speaker norms (i.e. speak like native speakers) high levels of proficiency ensue, but when the conditions encourage learners to maintain their own social ingroup less learning takes place. According to Giles's theory, then, social factors influence interlanguage development via the impact they have on the attitudes that determine the kinds of language use learners engage in.

Accommodation theory suggests that social factors, mediated through the interactions that learners take part in, influence both how quickly they learn and the actual route that they follow. This latter claim is controversial, however, as it suggests that sequences of acquisition are not as fixed as many researchers have claimed.

The acculturation model of L2 acquisition

A similar perspective on the role of social factors in L2 acquisition can be found in John Schumann's **acculturation model**. This model, which has been highly influential, is built around the metaphor of 'distance'.

The theory originated in a case study. Schumann investigated a thirty-three-year-old Costa Rican named Alberto, who was acquiring English in the United States. Schumann found very little evidence of any linguistic development in Alberto over a ten-month period. Alberto used a 'reduced and simplified form of English' throughout. For example, he did not progress beyond the first stage in the development of negatives (i.e. the use of '*no* + verb' constructions), he continued to use declarative word order rather than inversion in questions (for example, 'Where you get that?'), he acquired virtually no auxiliary verbs, and he failed to mark regular verbs for past tense or nouns for possession. The grammatical features that he did seem to have acquired (for example, plural *-s* and copula *is*) could be accounted for by positive transfer from his native language, Spanish. In short, Alberto appeared to have fossilized, or as Schumann put it 'pidginized', at a very early stage of development.

Why was this? Schumann entertained a number of possible reasons—for example, intelligence and age—and dismissed all of them. This led him to consider whether the reasons that have been advanced for the formation of a pidgin (i.e. a very simple contact language used among speakers who have no common language) might also apply to L2 acquisition. Schumann proposed that **pidginization** in L2 acquisition results when learners fail to acculturate to the target-language group, that is, when they are unable or unwilling to adapt to a new culture.

The main reason for learners failing to acculturate is **social distance**. This concerns the extent to which individual learners become members of a target-language group and therefore achieve contact with them. A learner's social distance is determined by a number of factors. Thus, a 'good' learning situation is one where there is little social distance because the target-language group and the L2 group view each other as socially equal, both groups wish the L2 group to assimilate the target-language group and the L2 group share the same social facilities, the L2 group lacks cohesion (i.e. has many contacts with the target-language group), the L2 group is small, both groups display positive attitudes towards each other, and the L2 group is relatively permanent. Schumann also recognizes that social distance is sometimes indeterminate. In such cases, he suggests **psychological distance** becomes important and identifies a further set of psychological factors, such as language shock and motivation, to account for this.

As presented by Schumann, social factors determine the amount of contact with the L2 individual learners experience and thereby how successful they are in learning. There are two problems with such a model. First, it fails to acknowledge that factors like 'integration pattern' and 'attitude' are not fixed and static but, potentially, variable and dynamic, fluctuating in accordance with the learner's changing social experiences. Second, it fails to acknowledge that learners are not just subject *to* social conditions but can also become the subject *of* them; they can help to construct the social context of their own learning. It is this notion that we will now explore.

Social identity and investment in L2 learning

The notions of 'subject to' and 'subject of' are central to Bonny Peirce's view of the relationship between social context and L2 acquisition. She illustrates this neatly with an extract from the diary of Eva, an adult immigrant learner of English in Canada:

> The girl which is working with me pointed at the man and said: 'Do you see him?'—I said
> 'Yes. Why?'
> 'Don't you know him?'
> 'No. I don't know him.'
> 'How come you don't know him? Don't you watch TV? That's Bart Simpson.'
> It made me feel so bad and I didn't answer her nothing.
>
> (from B.N. Peirce. 1995. 'Social identity, investment, and language learning.' *TESOL Quarterly* 29:9–31)

Eva felt humiliated in this conversation because she found herself positioned as a 'strange woman', someone who did not know who Bart Simpson was. She was subject to a discourse which assumed an identity she did not have. As Peirce points out, Eva could have made herself the subject of the discourse had she attempted to reshape the grounds on which the interaction took place, for example, by asserting that she did not watch the kind of TV programmes of which Bart Simpson was the star. However, in this instance Eva did not feel able to assert such an identity for herself.

The notion of social identity is central to the theory Peirce advances. She argues that language learners have complex social identities that can only be understood in terms of the power relations that shape social structures. A learner's social identity is, according to Peirce, 'multiple and contradictory'. Learning is successful when learners are able to summon up or construct an identity that enables them to impose their right to be heard and thus become the subject of the discourse. This requires **investment**, something learners will only make if they believe their efforts will increase the value of their 'cultural capital' (i.e. give them access to the knowledge and modes of thought that will enable them to function successfully in a variety of social contexts).

Peirce's social theory of L2 acquisition affords a different set of metaphors. L2 acquisition involves a 'struggle' and 'investment'. Learners are not computers who process input data but combatants who battle to assert themselves and investors who expect a good return on their efforts. Successful learners are those who reflect critically on how they engage with native speakers and who are prepared to challenge the accepted social order by constructing and asserting social identities of their own choice.

Socio-cultural models of L2 acquisition, such as those of Giles, Schumann, and Peirce, are intended to account for learners' relative success or failure in learning an L2. That is, they seek to explain the speed of learning and the ultimate level of proficiency of different groups of learners. The models assume settings where the target language is used for everyday communication. In such situations social conditions determine the extent of learners' contact with the L2 and their commitment to learning it. However, socio-cultural models may be less relevant to foreign language settings where most learners' principal contact with the L2 is in a classroom.

5
Discourse aspects of interlanguage

Social factors do not impact directly on what goes on inside the 'black box'. Rather they have an indirect effect, influencing the communication learners engage in and through this the rate and possibly the route of interlanguage development. We need to consider, then, what the nature of this communication is and how it affects L2 acquisition. To this end we will now focus our attention on the discourse in which learners participate.

The study of learner discourse in SLA has been informed by two rather different goals. On the one hand there have been attempts to discover how L2 learners acquire the 'rules' of discourse that inform native-speaker language use. This work is analogous to the work on the acquisition of grammar (see Chapter 2) and is essentially descriptive in nature. On the other hand, a number of researchers have sought to show how interaction shapes interlanguage development (i.e. how discourse influences the kinds of errors learners make and the developmental orders and sequences they pass through). This work is explanatory and will be our major concern here. First, however, we will briefly consider some of the descriptive work on learner discourse.

Acquiring discourse rules

There are rules or, at least, regularities in the ways in which native speakers hold conversations. In the United States, for example, a compliment usually calls for a response and failure to provide one can be considered a sociolinguistic error. Furthermore, in American English compliment responses are usually quite elaborate, involving some attempt on the part of the speaker to play down the compliment by making some unfavourable comment. For example:

A: I like your sweater.
B: It's so old. My sister bought it for me in Italy some time ago.

However, L2 learners behave differently. Sometimes they fail to respond to a compliment at all. At other times they produce bare responses (for example, 'Thank you').

There is a growing body of research investigating learner discourse. This shows that, to some extent at least, the acquisition of discourse rules, like the acquisition of grammatical rules, is systematic, reflecting both distinct types of errors and developmental sequences. We saw evidence of this in the clear developmental pattern evident in how J and R learned to make requests (see Chapter 1). However, more work is needed to demonstrate which aspects are universal and which are language specific as it is already clear that many aspects of learner discourse are influenced by the rules of discourse in the learner's L1. We will later examine how learners transfer discourse features from their L1 to the L2.

The role of input and interaction in L2 acquisition

The bulk of the research on learner discourse has been concerned with whether and how input and interaction affect L2 acquisition. A number of rather different theoretical positions can be identified. As we have already seen, a behaviourist view treats language learning as environmentally determined, controlled from the outside by the stimuli learners are exposed to and the reinforcement they receive. In contrast, mentalist theories emphasize the importance of the learner's 'black box'. They maintain that learners' brains are especially equipped to learn language and all that is needed is minimal exposure to input in order to trigger acquisition. Interactionist theories of L2 acquisition acknowledge the importance of both input and internal language processing. Learning takes place as a result of a complex interaction between the linguistic environment and the learner's internal mechanisms.

As we have already seen, the behaviourist view has been largely discredited. We will examine the mentalist position more fully later. For now, we will focus on the interactionist perspective.

One question that can be asked is whether the discourse in which learners participate is in any way different from the discourse native speakers engage in. If learner discourse can be shown to have special properties it is possible that these contribute to acquisition in some way.

It does indeed have special properties. Just as caretakers modify the way they speak to children learning their L1, so do native speakers modify their speech when communicating with learners. These modifications are evident in both input and interaction. Input modifications have been investigated through the study of **foreigner talk**, the language that native speakers use when addressing non-native speakers. Two types of foreigner talk can be identified—ungrammatical and grammatical. Examples of these are provided in Table 5.1.

Ungrammatical foreigner talk is socially marked. It often implies a lack of respect on the part of the native speaker and can be resented by learners. Ungrammatical foreigner talk is characterized by the deletion of certain grammatical features such as copula *be*, modal verbs (for example, *can* and *must*) and articles, the use of the base form of the verb in place of the past tense form, and the use of special constructions such as '*no* + verb'. It should be immediately apparent that these features are the same as those commonly found in learners' interlanguages. This raises the intriguing possibility that, contrary to the view presented earlier, interlanguage forms are, in fact, learned from the input. However, this is unlikely, as learners who experience grammatical foreigner talk still manifest the same interlanguage errors as those that experience ungrammatical foreigner talk. There is no convincing evidence that learners' errors derive from the language they are exposed to.

Grammatical foreigner talk is the norm. Various types of modification of baseline talk (i.e. the kind of talk native speakers address to other native speakers) can be identified. First, grammatical foreigner talk is delivered at a slower pace. Second, the input is simplified. Examples of simplifications in the grammatical foreigner talk shown in Table 5.1 are the use of shorter sentences, avoidance of subordinate clauses, and the omission of complex grammatical forms like question tags. Third, grammatical foreigner talk is sometimes regularized. This involves the use of forms that are in some sense 'regular' or 'basic'. An example in Table 5.1 is the use of a full rather than a contracted form ('will not forget' instead of 'won't forget'). Fourth, foreigner talk sometimes consists of elaborated language use. This involves the lengthening of phrases and sentences in order to make the meaning clearer. An example of elaboration in Table 5.1 is the use of 'when you are coming home' as a paraphrase of 'on your way home'.

Type of talk	Example
Baseline talk	You won't forget to buy the ice-cream on your way home, will you?
Ungrammatical foreigner talk	No forget buying ice-cream, eh?
Grammatical foreigner talk	The ice-cream—You will not forget to buy it on your way home—Get it when you are coming home. All right?

TABLE 5.1 *Examples of baseline and foreigner talk*

Input modifications of these kinds originate in the person addressing a learner. We seem to know intuitively how to modify the way we talk to learners to make it easier for them to understand. However, there are times when learners still fail to understand. When this happens they have a choice. They can pretend they have understood. Research shows that learners sometimes do this. Alternatively, learners can signal that they have not understood. This results in interactional modifications as the participants in the discourse engage in the **negotiation of meaning**. The extract below is an example of an exchange between two learners. Izumi uses a confirmation check ('in him knee') to make sure she has understood Hiroko when he said 'in his knee'. In so doing she introduces an error of her own which leads Hiroko to correct it at the same time as he corrects his own original error 'on his knee'. As a result of this negotiation both learners end up correcting their own errors. There is plenty of evidence to suggest that modified interaction of this kind is common in learner discourse.

> Hiroko: A man is uh. drinking c-coffee or tea with uh the saucer of the uh uh coffee set is uh in his uh knee.
> Izumi: in him knee.
> Hiroko: uh on his knee.
> Izumi: yeah
> Hiroko: on *his* knee
> Izumi: so sorry. on *his* knee.

(from S. Gass and E. Varonis. 1994. 'Input, interaction and second language production.' *Studies in Second Language Acquisition* 16:283–302)

How do such input and interactional modifications contribute to L2 acquisition? There is still only limited empirical evidence that these modifications do assist interlanguage development. Arguments have been proposed, however, that suggest they do.

According to Stephen Krashen's **input hypothesis,** L2 acquisition takes place when a learner understands input that contains grammatical forms that are at 'i + 1' (i.e. are a little more advanced than the current state of the learner's interlanguage). Krashen suggests that the right level of input is attained automatically when interlocutors succeed in making themselves understood in communication. Success is achieved by using the situational context to make messages clear and through the kinds of input modifications found in foreigner talk. According to Krashen, then, L2 acquisition depends on **comprehensible input.**

Michael Long's **interaction hypothesis** also emphasizes the importance of comprehensible input but claims that it is most effective when it is modified through the negotiation of meaning. It is not difficult to see why. As the interaction between Hiroko and Izumi illustrates, learners often receive **negative evidence.** That is, their interlocutors indicate when they have not understood and, in the course of so doing, may model the correct target-language forms. Thus, learners receive input relevant to aspects of grammar that they have not yet fully mastered. There is another way in which interaction may assist learners. When learners have the chance to clarify something that has been said they are giving themselves more time to process the input, which may help them not just to comprehend but also to acquire new L2 forms. However, sometimes interaction can overload learners with input, as when a speaker provides lengthy paraphrases or long definitions of unknown words. In such cases, acquisition may be impeded rather than facilitated. The relationship between modified interaction and L2 acquisition is clearly a complex one.

Another perspective on the relationship between discourse and L2 acquisition is provided by Evelyn Hatch. Hatch emphasizes the collaborative endeavours of the learners and their interlocutors in constructing discourse and suggests that syntactic structures can grow out of the process of building discourse. One way in which this can occur is through **scaffolding**. Learners use the discourse to help them produce utterances that they would not be able to produce on their own, as in this example from Wagner Gough:

Mark: Come here.
Homer: No come here.

Homer, the L2 learner, produces a negative utterance with the common '*no* + verb' pattern by repeating his interlocutor's utterance and attaching the negator *no* at the front. Scaffolding of this type is common in the early stages of L2 acquisition and may account for some of the early transitional structures that have been observed in interlanguage.

Other SLA theorists have drawn on the theories of L.S. Vygotsky, a Russian psychologist, to explain how interaction serves as the bedrock of acquisition. The two key constructs in what is known as 'activity theory', based on Vygotsky's ideas, are 'motive' and 'internalization'. The first concerns the active way in which individuals define the goals of an activity for themselves by deciding what to attend to and what not to attend to. The second concerns how a novice comes to solve a problem with the assistance of an 'expert', who provides 'scaffolding', and then internalizes the solution. In this respect, the notion of the **zone of proximal development** is important. Vygotsky argues that children learn through interpersonal activity, such as play with adults, whereby they form concepts that would be beyond them if they were acting alone. In other words, zones of proximal development are created through interaction with more knowledgeable others. Subsequently, the child learns how to control a concept without the assistance of others. Seen this way, development manifests itself first in social interaction and only later inside the learner. According to activity theory, socially constructed L2 knowledge is a necessary condition for interlanguage development.

The negotiation of meaning illustrated in the exchange between Hiroko and Izumi and the discourse scaffolding which Hatch and others have observed can both be interpreted as evidence of the applicability of Vygotsky's ideas about cognitive development in children to L2 acquisition.

The role of output in L2 acquisition

So far we have concentrated on the roles of input and interaction in L2 acquisition, but we also need to consider whether output plays any part in interlanguage development. After all, discourse supplies learners with the opportunity to produce language as well as hear it. Here we find conflicting opinions. Krashen argues that 'speaking is the result of acquisition not its cause'. He claims that the only way learners can learn from their output is by treating it as **auto-input**. In effect, Krashen is refuting the cherished belief of many teachers that languages are learned by practising them. In contrast, Merrill Swain has argued that comprehensible output also plays a part in L2 acquisition. She suggests a number of specific ways in which learners can learn from their own output. Output can serve a consciousness-raising function by helping learners to notice gaps in their interlanguages. That is, by trying to speak or write in the L2 they realize that they lack the grammatical knowledge of some feature that is important for what they want to say. Second, output helps learners to test hypotheses. They can try out a rule and see whether it leads to successful communication or whether it elicits negative feedback. Third, learners sometimes talk about their own output, identifying problems with it and discussing ways in which they can be put right.

Summary

In this chapter we have considered a number of ways in which discourse might contribute to L2 acquisition—through the modified input that comes in foreigner talk, through the input learners obtain from the negotiation of meaning, through scaffolding, and through comprehensible output. In the various positions we have examined we find a rich array of metaphors on offer. In particular, there are metaphors that suggest that L2 acquisition is a distinctively human and social activity (for example, 'negotiation' and 'collaboration'). The underlying metaphor that informs work on discourse in SLA, however, remains that of the computer (for example, in the choice of basic terms like 'input' and 'output'). We shall now look inside the computer and examine some of the mental mechanisms of L2 acquisition.

6
Psycholinguistic aspects of interlanguage

Psycholinguistics is the study of the mental structures and processes involved in the acquisition and use of language. The study of psycholinguistic aspects of L2 acquisition has been prominent in SLA and has given rise to many acquisition models. Here we will focus on a small number of major issues—**L1 transfer**, the role of consciousness, processing operations, and **communication strategies**.

L1 transfer

L1 transfer refers to the influence that the learner's L1 exerts over the acquisition of an L2. This influence is apparent in a number of ways. First, as we noted in the section on error analysis in Chapter 2, the learner's L1 is one of the sources of error in learner language. This influence is referred to as **negative transfer**. However, in some cases, the learner's L1 can facilitate L2 acquisition. For example, French learners of English are much less likely to make errors of this kind:

The man whom I spoke to him is a millionaire.

than are Arabic learners because French does not permit resumptive pronouns (like 'him') in relative clauses whereas Arabic does. This type of effect is known as **positive transfer.**

L1 transfer can also result in **avoidance**. For example, Chinese and Japanese learners of English have been found to avoid the use of relative clauses because their languages do not contain equivalent structures. These learners make fewer errors in relative clauses than Arabic learners of English but only because they rarely use them. Finally, L1 transfer may be reflected in the **overuse** of some forms. For example, some Chinese learners tend to overuse expressions of regret when apologizing in English, in accordance with the norms of their mother tongue.

Theoretical accounts of L1 transfer have undergone considerable revision since the early days of SLA. In the heyday of behaviourism it was believed that errors were largely the result of interference (another term for negative transfer). That is, the habits of the L1 were supposed to prevent the learner from learning the habits of the L2. In the belief that interference, and thereby learning difficulty, could be predicted by identifying those areas of the target language that were different from the learners' L1, comparisons of the two languages were carried out using **contrastive analysis**. The resulting list of differences was used to make decisions about the content of teaching materials.

As we have already seen, behaviourist theories cannot adequately account for L2 acquisition and they fell out of favour in the early 1970s. This led to two developments. Some theorists, espousing strong mentalist accounts of L2 acquisition, sought to play down the role of the L1. They argued that very few errors were the result of L1 transfer. An analysis of the errors produced by Spanish learners of L2 English, for example, led one pair of researchers to claim that less than 5 per cent of the errors were the result of transfer. This minimalist view of L1 transfer, however, has not withstood the test of time.

The second development was to reconceptualize transfer within a cognitive framework. This was begun by Larry Selinker. In his formulation of interlanguage theory he identified language transfer as one of the mental processes responsible for fossilization. Subsequently, there has been widespread acknowledgement that learners draw on their L1 in forming interlanguage hypotheses. Learners do not construct rules in a vacuum; rather they work with whatever information is at their disposal. This includes knowledge of their L1. The L1 can be viewed as a kind of 'input from the inside'. According to this view, then, transfer is not 'interference' but a cognitive process.

One of the main objections to a behaviourist account of L1 transfer is that transfer errors do not always occur when they are predicted to occur. That is, differences between the target and native languages do not always result in learning difficulty. Whereas a behaviourist theory cannot easily account for this, a cognitive theory, which recognizes that transfer will occur under some conditions but not under others, can do so. SLA has succeeded in identifying some of the cognitive constraints that govern the transfer of L1 knowledge. We will consider two of these constraints; learners' perceptions of what is transferable and their stage of development.

According to Eric Kellerman, learners have perceptions regarding the linguistic features of their own language. They treat some features as potentially transferable and others as potentially non-transferable. Broadly speaking, then, learners have a sense of what features in their L1 are in some way basic. They are more prepared to risk transferring such features than they are those they perceive to be unique to their own language. Kellerman found that advanced Dutch learners of English had clear perceptions about which meanings of 'breken' ('break') were basic in their L1 and which were unique. He also found that they were prepared to translate a sentence like:

Hij brak zijn been. (He broke his leg.)

directly into English, using 'broke' for '*brak*' but were not prepared to give a direct translation of a sentence like:

Het ondergrondse verset werd gebroken. (The underground resistance was broken.)

even though this was, in fact, possible. In other words, the learners transferred a basic meaning of '*breken*' but resisted transferring a meaning they perceived as unique.

The learner's stage of development has also been found to influence L1 transfer. This is clearly evident in the way learners acquire **speech acts** like requests, apologies, and refusals. Learners do not initially try to transfer their L1 speech-act strategies but, instead, rely on a few simple formulas. Thus, J and R (see Chapter 1) relied primarily on direct requests involving imperative verbs and the formula 'Can I have a ____?' Later, however, as learners' L2 proficiency develops, they may try to find ways of performing speech acts that accord with L1 norms. For example, in refusing invitations proficient Japanese speakers of English sometimes try to copy the high level of formality required in Japanese.

Other researchers have found that the transfer of some L1 grammatical features is tied to the learners' stage of development. For example, German and Norwegian learners of English, whose L1s manifest post-verbal negation (i.e. the negator is placed after the main verb rather than before as in '*Er geht nicht*' (literally 'He goes not'), do not initially transfer this feature into English. Instead they manifest pre-verbal negation like all other learners (for example, 'I no go'). Later, however, transfer of the L1 pattern takes place (for example, 'I go not'). This occurs when they learn that English does permit post-verbal negation with copula *be* (for example, 'She is not here').

It is clear, then, that transfer is governed by learners' perceptions about what is transferable and by their stage of development. It follows that interlanguage development cannot constitute a **restructuring continuum**. That is, the starting point is not the learners' L1, and learners do not proceed by replacing L1 rules with L2 rules. Rather they construct their own interim rules. However, they may well try to make use of their L1 knowledge along the way, but only when they believe it will help them in the learning task or when they have become sufficiently proficient in the L2 for transfer to be possible.

'Transfer' is yet another metaphor for explaining L2 acquisition. In some ways it is an inappropriate one. When we transfer money we move it out of one account and into another, so one account gains and the other loses. However, when language transfer takes place there is usually no loss of L1 knowledge. This obvious fact has led to the suggestion that a better term for referring to the effects of the L1 might be 'cross-linguistic influence'.

The role of consciousness in L2 acquisition

When children acquire their L1 they seem to do so without conscious effort. In contrast, L2 learners, especially adults, seem to have to work hard and to study the language consciously in order to succeed. This comparison is not entirely accurate, however, for L2 learners, even adult ones, are also capable of 'picking up' language in much the same way as children do in L1 acquisition. At stake here is one of the most controversial issues in SLA—the role of consciousness.

Two opposing positions can be identified. Stephen Krashen has argued the need to distinguish 'acquired' L2 knowledge (i.e. implicit knowledge *of* the language) and 'learned' L2 knowledge (i.e. explicit knowledge *about* language). He claims that the former is developed subconsciously through comprehending input while communicating, while the latter is developed consciously through deliberate study of the L2. However, as we will shortly see, this claim is controversial. So, too, is Krashen's claim that the two knowledge systems are entirely independent of one another and that 'learned' knowledge can never be converted into 'acquired' knowledge. This contradicts skill-building theories of L2 acquisition, according to which learners can achieve grammatical accuracy by automatizing 'learned' knowledge through practice.

Richard Schmidt has pointed out that the term 'consciousness' is often used very loosely in SLA and argues that there is a need to standardize the concepts that underlie its use. For example, he distinguishes between consciousness as 'intentionality' and consciousness as 'attention'. 'Intentionality' refers to whether a learner makes a conscious and deliberate decision to learn some L2 knowledge. It contrasts with 'incidental learning', which takes place when learners pick up L2 knowledge through exposure. Schmidt argues that no matter whether learning is intentional or incidental, it involves conscious attention to features in the input.

This distinction is important and helpful. It helps us to see that when Krashen talks about 'acquisition' being 'incidental' and 'subconscious' he has failed to recognize that 'incidental' acquisition might in fact still involve some degree of conscious 'attention' to input. In other words, learning incidentally is not the same as learning without conscious attention.

There are, in fact, very different positions regarding the need for conscious attention in L2 acquisition. Schmidt argues that learning cannot take place without what he calls **noticing**—the process of attending consciously to linguistic features in the input. He provides evidence of the importance of noticing in a study of his own acquisition of Portuguese when he was in Brazil. Schmidt kept a diary, recording the various L2 features he noticed in the input he experienced. Subsequent analyses of his output showed that in nearly every case the forms that he produced were those that he had previously noticed people using when they spoke to him. At best, however, this constitutes limited evidence of the need for conscious attention. Other researchers, not least Krashen, have resisted the claim that input processing involves noticing.

Schmidt also points to a third sense in which we can talk about consciousness in language learning. He uses the term 'awareness' to refer to whether learners are conscious of acquiring new L2 elements (i.e. of when 'intake' is converted into L2 knowledge—see Figure 3.1). The possibility of learning taking place implicitly in this way is even more hotly disputed. According to some psychologists, learners can achieve long-term storage of complex material through implicit learning. That is, they can learn without awareness and without consciously testing hypotheses. However, other psychologists have disputed this, arguing that the learning which has taken place only *appears* to be implicit but, in fact, learners are aware of what they are learning.

Irrespective of whether learners learn implicitly or explicitly, it is widely accepted that they can acquire different kinds of knowledge. It is perhaps self-evident that all language users, including L2 learners, *know* rules that guide their performance without any awareness of what the rules consist of. Of course, they can always reflect on this **implicit knowledge**, thus making it explicit. It is also clear that L2 learners may have knowledge *about* the L2 (i.e. **explicit knowledge**) but be unable to use this knowledge in performance without conscious attention. Given the validity of the distinction between implicit and explicit knowledge, two questions can be posed; what is the extent of learners' explicit L2 knowledge and what part does it play in the acquisition of implicit knowledge?

Little is actually known about the nature of learners' explicit L2 knowledge. Krashen's view is that most learners are only capable of learning fairly simple rules. An example of a simple rule in English is plural -s, while an example of a complex rule is that pertaining to the use of articles, *a* and *the*. An alternative view, which has been supported by research, is that some learners may be capable of learning substantial amounts of explicit knowledge. In such cases, however, their explicit knowledge is not always very accurate.

Explicit knowledge may aid learners in developing implicit knowledge in a number of ways. First, contrary to the claims of Krashen, a direct interface may occur. However, as we shall see later in Chapter 9, this seems to be developmentally regulated; in other words, explicit knowledge may only convert into implicit knowledge when learners are at the right stage of development. Second, explicit knowledge may facilitate the process by which learners attend to features in the input. For example, a learner who knows *about* the subjunctive in French is better equipped to notice it. Third, explicit knowledge may help learners to move from intake to acquisition by helping them to **notice the gap** between what they have observed in the input and the current state of their interlanguage as manifested in their own output. Schmidt found that noticing the gap was characteristic of his acquisition of Portuguese. Thus, even if explicit knowledge does not contribute directly to the development of implicit knowledge it may do so indirectly by helping learners to process input and intake.

Processing operations

Another way of identifying the processes responsible for interlanguage development is to deduce the operations that learners perform from a close inspection of their output. This approach, which belongs to the mainstream of SLA in that it focuses close attention on learner language, has afforded a number of proposals. We shall examine two of them here; operating principles and processing constraints.

Operating principles

The study of the L1 acquisition of many different languages has led to the identification of a number of general strategies which children use to extract and segment linguistic information from the language they hear. Dan Slobin has referred to these strategies as **operating principles**. Examples are 'avoid interruption and rearrangement of linguistic units' and 'avoid exceptions'. It is not difficult to see how such principles apply to L2 acquisition. For example, learners of L2 English produce errors like:

My brother made me to give him some money.

The verb 'make' takes the base form of the verb (i.e. in this example 'give') as its complement rather than an infinitive (i.e. 'to give') which most other verbs in English take. It constitutes, therefore, an exception to a general rule. Thus, when learners use an infinitive with 'make', they are avoiding this problem.

Roger Andersen describes a number of operating principles for L2 acquisition. These are based on the detailed analysis of the language produced by learners of L2 English and L2 Spanish. Andersen claims that his principles are 'macro principles', each one relating to a group of principles in Slobin's more detailed framework. An example of a macro principle is 'the one-to-one principle' according to which learners seek to map a single meaning onto a single form. This principle accounts for why J sought to use '*no* + verb' negatives to perform statements and '*don't* + verb' negatives to perform commands (see page 28).

Operating principles provide a simple and attractive way of accounting for the properties of interlanguage. However, they have been criticized on a number of grounds. It is not clear how many principles are needed and the ones that have been advanced are not mutually exclusive. More important, perhaps, is the absence of any overarching theory to explain where the principles themselves come from.

Processing constraints

A project known as ZISA (*Zweitspracherwerb Italienischer und Spanischer Arbeiter*) investigated the order in which migrant workers with Romance language backgrounds acquired a number of German word-order rules. The project found clear evidence of a developmental route, bearing out the research on acquisitional patterns we examined in Chapter 2.

What distinguishes this work on acquisitional sequences is that it led to and was informed by a strong theory, known as the **multidimensional model**. This theory sought to account for both why learners acquire the grammar of a language in a definite order and also why some learners only develop very simple interlanguage grammars.

The theory proposes that some grammatical features, such as the word-order rules referred to above, are acquired in sequence while others, such as copula *be*, can be acquired at any stage of development. Thus, it distinguishes a developmental and a variational axis. Progress along one axis is independent of progress along the other axis.

To account for progress along the developmental axis a number of **processing constraints** have been proposed. These govern when it is possible for a learner to move from one stage to another. For example, learners begin by adopting the 'canonical order strategy'. This prevents them from interrupting the basic subject–verb–object word order. Later they develop the 'initialization/finalization strategy' which enables them to move elements at the end of a structure to the beginning and vice versa but prevents them moving elements within a structure. For example, mastery of this strategy enables learners to place an adverb at the beginning of a sentence:

Gestern ich gehe ins Kino. (Yesterday I go to the cinema.)

but prevents them from inverting the subject and verb (which is required in German, as in this sentence):

Gestern gehe ich ins Kino. (Yesterday go I to the cinema.)

Later, learners achieve access to the 'subordinate clause strategy', which permits movement of elements within main clauses but blocks them in subordinate clauses. Learners who have developed this strategy can now invert subject and verb after an adverb but still cannot move the verb to the end of subordinate clause. These strategies capture what learners can do at different stages in their development and, also, what 'blocks' they must overcome to develop further. Progress consists of the removal of first one and then another of these blocks.

Movement along the variational axis, it is claimed, is determined by socio-psychological factors. Learners who want to integrate into the target-language community progress rapidly along this axis. However, learners who want to maintain their own separate identities progress more slowly and sometimes not at all. This seems to correspond closely to Giles' idea of accommodation and Schumann's idea of acculturation (see page 39).

The multidimensional model is a powerful theory of L2 acquisition in that it proposes mechanisms to account for why learners follow a definite acquisitional route. However, the model has also been subject to considerable criticism. It has been pointed out that it is based on research into a fairly limited set of grammatical features. It is also not clear how variational features can be identified and, in fact, few examples have been provided, the most frequently mentioned being copula *be*. More seriously, the model provides no account of how or why the 'blocks' to developmental progress are removed. The metaphor of 'blocks' is interesting but remains rather undeveloped.

Communication strategies

So far we have focused on psycholinguistic accounts of how learners develop their interlanguages. Now we will take a brief look at the mechanisms involved when learners use the L2 knowledge they have acquired in communication.

As anyone who has tried to communicate in an L2 knows, learners frequently experience problems in saying what they want to say because of their inadequate knowledge. In order to overcome these problems they resort to various kinds of communication strategies. For example, they may avoid problematic items such as the verb 'make' (which, as we saw on page 58, is exceptional in taking a base form of the verb as its complement), by substituting an item like 'ask' (which is regular in that it takes *to* + infinitive and is therefore easier to use correctly). If learners do not know a word in the target language they may 'borrow' a word from their L1 or use another target-language word that is approximate in meaning (for example, 'worm' for 'silkworm'), or try to paraphrase the meaning of the word, or even construct an entirely new word (for example, 'picture place' for 'art gallery'). These strategies, with the obvious exception of those that are L1 based, are also found in the language use of native speakers.

There have been a number of attempts to construct psycholinguistic models to account for the use of communication strategies. Claus Færch and Gabriele Kasper, for example, proposed a model of speech production which involves a planning and an execution phase. Communication strategies are seen as part of the planning phase. They are called upon when learners experience some kind of problem with an initial plan which prevents them from executing it. They can either abandon the initial plan and develop an entirely different one by means of a reduction strategy (such as switching to a different topic) or try to maintain their original communicative goal by adopting some kind of achievement strategy (such as L1 borrowing).

As Selinker has pointed out, communication strategies constitute one of the processes responsible for learner errors. We might expect, therefore, that the choice of communication strategies will reflect the learners' stage of development. For example, learners might be expected to switch from L1-based strategies to L2-based strategies as their knowledge of the L2 develops. It would also be interesting to discover whether the use of communication strategies has any effect on L2 acquisition. For example, do learners notice the gap (see page 57) more readily as a result of having to use a communication strategy? Or does successful use of a communication strategy obviate the need for learners to learn the correct target-language forms? However, nothing is yet known about this.

Two types of computational model

In this chapter we have attempted to peer inside the 'black box' of the learner's brain in order to identify some of the mental processes involved in constructing and using an interlanguage. Of course, these processes cannot be viewed directly. They can only be inferred from the various behaviours learners engage in. What distinguishes a cognitive account from a behaviourist one is that an attempt is made to explain L2 acquisition in terms of mental processing.

As we have seen, the prevailing metaphor for explaining these processes has been that of the computer. The 'black box' houses some kind of apparatus that extracts information from the 'input', works on it, stores it, and subsequently uses it in 'output'. However, the actual type of apparatus involved and the nature of the computation performed remain a matter of some disagreement. In particular, two radically different types of apparatus have been proposed. One type involves the idea of 'serial processing'. That is, information is processed in a series of sequential steps and results in the representation of what has been learned as some kind of 'rule' or 'strategy'. This is the dominant version of the computational model in SLA and is evident in much of the preceding discussion. For example Færch and Kasper's model of speech production presupposes that communication problems are dealt with in sequential steps.

The alternative type of apparatus involves the idea of **parallel distributed processing**. This credits the learner with the ability to perform a number of mental tasks at the same time, for example, the ability to attend to both form and meaning while processing input. Models based on parallel distributed processing reject the whole notion of 'rule'. Instead, they see mental structure as consisting of elaborate sets of weighted connections between separate items. For example, instead of accounting for the regular past tense in terms of a general rule (add *-ed* to the base form of the verb), we might envisage a mental network in which individual verbs are connected more or less strongly to *-ed*. Such a model helps to explain why some verbs are regularly used with *-ed*, some are sometimes used, and some never. Not surprisingly, parallel distributed processing is controversial as it constitutes an affront to one of the central precepts of linguistics, namely that language is rule-governed.

7
Linguistic aspects of interlanguage

In Chapter 6 we examined some of the cognitive structures involved in interlanguage development. To provide another perspective on L2 acquisition, we will now consider how the nature of the object to be acquired—language—influences development. This ties SLA to the discipline of linguistics.

Typological universals: relative clauses

A good example of how linguistic enquiry can shed light on interlanguage development can be found in the study of relative clauses. As we have seen, languages vary in whether they have relative clause structures. Some languages, like English and Arabic, have them, while other languages, like Chinese and Japanese, do not. This linguistic difference influences the ease with which learners are able to learn relative clauses. Learners whose L1 includes relative clauses find them easier to learn than learners whose L1 does not and, consequently, they are less likely to avoid learning them.

The linguistic properties of relative clauses affect L2 acquisition in another way. In languages like English, a relative clause can be attached to the end of a matrix clause:

The police have caught the man *who bombed the hotel.*

or they can be embedded in the main clause:

The man *who bombed the hotel* has been caught by the police.

When learners of L2 English begin to acquire relative clauses they typically begin with the first type. Thus, the linguistic structure of

English (i.e. the fact that relative clauses may or may not interrupt the main clause) influences how acquisition proceeds.

A third effect of relative clause structure on L2 acquisition can be identified. Linguists have shown that languages are more likely to permit relative clauses with a subject pronoun (for example, 'who') than with an object pronoun (for example, 'whom'). In fact, a hierarchy of relativization, known as the **accessibility hierarchy,** has been identified. This is illustrated in Table 7.1 for English, which, unlike many other languages, permits the full range of relative pronoun functions. The accessibility hierarchy is implicational in the sense that the presence of a relative pronoun function low in the order in a particular language implies the presence of all the pronoun functions above it but not those below it. For example, any language that permits the direct object function will necessarily permit the subject function but may not allow the indirect object function.

Relative pronoun function	Example
Subject	The writer *who won the Booker prize* is my lifelong friend.
Direct object	The writer *whom we met* won the Booker prize.
Indirect object	The writer *to whom I introduced you* won the Booker prize.
Object of preposition	The writer *with whom we had dinner* won the Booker prize.
Genitive	The writer *whose wife we met* won the Booker prize.
Object of comparative	The writer *who I have written more books than* has won the Booker prize.

TABLE 7.1 *The accessibility hierarchy for relative clauses*

Drawing on the accessibility hierarchy, SLA researchers have asked 'Does the hierarchy predict the order of acquisition of relative clauses?' There is some evidence that it does. For example, it has been found that the hierarchy predicts the frequency with which learners make errors in relative clauses, fewest errors being apparent in relative clauses with subject pronouns and most in clauses with the object of comparative function.

However, rather mixed results have been obtained for the genitive function. This has led to proposals that genitive relative clauses are not part of a single hierarchy but rather constitute a distinct hierarchy of their own. Whereas genitive structures may be more difficult to learn than non-genitive structures overall, some genitive structures are more difficult than others, the difficulty proving predictable on the basis of a separate hierarchy for genitives.

The accessibility hierarchy serves as an example of how SLA and linguistics can assist each other. On the one hand, linguistic facts can be used to explain and even predict acquisition. On the other, the results of empirical studies of L2 acquisition can be used to refine our understanding of linguistic facts.

Universal Grammar

SLA also owes a considerable debt to another branch of linguistics—that associated closely with Noam Chomsky's theory of **Universal Grammar (UG)**. Chomsky argues that language is governed by a set of highly abstract principles that provide parameters which are given particular settings in different languages.

Let us consider an example. A general principle of language is that it permits co-reference by means of some form of reflexive. Thus, in the English sentence:

The actress blamed herself.

the subject, 'actress', is co-referential with the reflexive, 'herself' in the sense that both words refer to the same person. However, reflexives also vary cross-linguistically. In the case of English, a reflexive can only co-refer to a subject within the same clause, as in the example above. Thus, English only permits 'local binding'. 'Long-distance binding', where the reflexive co-refers to a subject in another clause, is prohibited. Thus, in this sentence:

Emily knew the actress would blame herself.

the reflexive must be understood as referring to 'actress' and not to 'Emily'. However, other languages such as Japanese, permit long-distance as well as local binding. Thus, the Japanese version of the sentence above is ambiguous; the reflexive can refer to either the actress or to Emily.

What is the significance of such linguistic information for L2 acquisition? Clearly, Japanese learners of L2 English need to learn that reflexives in English permit only local binding; they have to reset the parameter. A number of studies have investigated whether Japanese learners are able to do this. In one such study, Japanese learners of English of different proficiency levels were shown sentences like the one above and asked to state which noun the reflexive referred to. Overall the more proficient learners were no better at this than the less proficient ones, suggesting that the learners operated in accordance with their L1 setting of the parameter and that no resetting for English was taking place. Other studies, however, have provided evidence that Japanese learners can reset this parameter. The results provided by research are, therefore, inconclusive.

The question of whether learners whose L1 permits both local and long-distance binding of reflexives can learn that a language like English permits only local binding may seem a rather trivial matter. In fact, though, it concerns an issue of considerable theoretical importance—the extent to which a language other than our mother tongue is fully learnable.

Learnability

Chomsky has claimed that children learning their L1 must rely on innate knowledge of language because otherwise the task facing them is an impossible one. His argument is that the input to which children are exposed is insufficient to enable them to discover the rules of the language they are trying to learn. This insufficiency is referred to as the **poverty of the stimulus**. For example, a child learning English needs to discover that sentences like this are ungrammatical:

Sam kicked fiercely his toy car.

because English does not permit an adverb between the verb and the direct object. Can this be learned solely on the basis of input? The argument is that it cannot if the input consists only of **positive**

evidence (i.e. it provides information only about what *is* grammatical in the language) because learners can never be sure they will not hear a sentence where the adverb is between the verb and direct object. **Negative evidence** (i.e. input that provides direct evidence of what is ungrammatical in a language) would make it possible for children to find out that sentences like the one above are ungrammatical. However, children typically receive only positive evidence; their parents do not generally correct their grammatical mistakes. Thus, it is argued, the input seriously underdetermines learning. In other words, it does not provide the information needed for learning to be successful.

In the case of L1 acquisition, then, there is a logical problem. How do children invariably learn the full grammar of their mother tongue when the information they need is not always available in the input? The answer, according to Chomsky, is that children must have prior knowledge of what is grammatically possible and impossible and that this is part of their biological endowment. This knowledge, which in earlier formulations of the theory was referred to as the Language Acquisition Device (see page 32), is what comprises Universal Grammar (UG). It is claimed that some errors, such as the one involving adverb placement, simply do not occur in L1 acquisition because they are prohibited by UG.

But is this also the case in L2 acquisition? To answer this question we need to consider whether adult L2 learners have continued access to UG or whether they rely on some other kind of learning mechanism. We will begin by considering whether access depends on the age of the learner.

The critical period hypothesis

The **critical period hypothesis** states that there is a period during which language acquisition is easy and complete (i.e. native-speaker ability is achieved) and beyond which it is difficult and typically incomplete. The hypothesis was grounded in research which showed that people who lost their linguistic capabilities, for example as a result of an accident, were able to regain them totally before puberty (about the age of twelve) but were unable to do so afterwards. It was subsequently supported by studies of people who had been deprived of the opportunity even to acquire an L1 as a child. For example, Genie was totally isolated in the early years of her life and consequently did not start learning language (English) until the age of thirteen. While she developed considerable communicative ability she failed to acquire many grammatical rules. In this respect she resembled Wes, the Japanese subject of the case study referred to in Chapter 1.

There is considerable evidence to support the claim that L2 learners who begin learning as adults are unable to achieve native-speaker competence in either grammar or pronunciation. Studies of immigrants in the United States show that if they arrive before puberty they go on to achieve much higher levels of grammatical proficiency than if they arrive after. Sometimes they become indistinguishable from native speakers. However, there does not appear to be a sudden cut-off age, beyond which full competence is impossible. Rather the capacity to achieve full competence seems to decline gradually, becoming complete by about the age of sixteen. Interestingly, age of arrival is a much better predictor of ultimate achievement than the number of years of exposure to the target language. In the case of pronunciation, the crucial age appears to be much earlier, possibly as early as six.

There is some evidence that not all learners are subject to critical periods. Some are able to achieve native-speaker ability from an adult start. In one case, Julie, an English woman, did not start learning Arabic until she was twenty-one years old but was found to perform like a native speaker on a variety of tests after she had lived in Cairo for twenty-six years.

However, the relative lack of success of most L2 learners in comparison to L1 learners suggests that there may be radical differences in the way first and second languages are acquired. These differences may be of many kinds. It is likely, for instance, that differences in the social conditions in which L1 and L2 learners learn have some kind of impact. L1 learners, for example, do not experience social distance. It is also possible that L1 and L2 acquisition draw on different learning mechanisms because most adult L2 learners no longer have access to UG.

Access to UG

There is, in fact, no agreement as to whether adult L2 learners have access to UG. We will briefly examine a number of theoretical positions.

1 *Complete access*

It is argued that learners begin with the parameter settings of their L1 but subsequently learn to switch to the L2 parameter settings. An assumption is that full target-language competence is possible and that there is no such thing as a critical period. Learners like Julie constitute evidence in favour of this position.

2 *No access*

The argument here is that UG is not available to adult L2 learners. They rely on general learning strategies. According to this position, L1 and L2 acquisition are fundamentally different. Adult L2 learners will normally not be able to achieve full competence and their interlanguages may manifest 'impossible' rules (i.e. rules that would be prohibited by UG).

3 *Partial access*

Another theoretical possibility is that learners have access to parts of UG but not others. For example, they may have access to only those UG parameters operative in their L1. However, they may be able to switch to the L2 parameter setting with the help of direct instruction involving error correction. In other words, L2 acquisition is partly regulated by UG and partly by general learning strategies.

4 *Dual access*

According to this position, adult L2 learners make use of both UG and general learning strategies. However, the use of general learning strategies can 'block' the operation of UG, causing learners to produce 'impossible' errors and to fail to achieve full competence. This position assumes that adult learners can only be fully successful providing they rely on UG.

The existence of such contradictory positions shows that the role of UG in L2 acquisition is still uncertain.

Markedness

This uncertainty regarding the contribution of linguistic theory to the study of L2 acquisition is also evident in another area of linguistic enquiry—the study of **markedness**.

This term refers to the general idea that some structures are more 'natural' or 'basic' than other structures. In typological linguistics, unmarked structures are those that are common in the world's languages. In Chomskyan linguistics, unmarked structures are those that are governed by UG and which, therefore require only minimal evidence for acquisition. Marked structures are those that lie outside UG (for example, have arisen as a result of historical accident). In addition, attempts have also been made to distinguish degrees of markedness in the different settings of a parameter of UG. For example, 'local binding' of reflexives is considered unmarked in relation to 'long-distance binding'.

A number of hypotheses relating to markedness have been examined in SLA. One is that learners acquire less marked structures before more marked ones. On the face of it, there is considerable evidence in support of this. For example, if the accessibility hierarchy is taken to reflect the degree of markedness of relative pronoun functions (see Table 7.1), then, clearly the degree of markedness correlates with the order of acquisition. However, there is a problem. We need to be sure that it is markedness and not some other factor that determines the order of acquisition. Learners may acquire the subject function first not because it is the least marked but because it is the most frequent in the input. To test whether it is markedness or input frequency which determines acquisition order we must identify unmarked and marked structures that are respectively less and more frequent in the input. Research completed to date suggests that learners are more likely to acquire a frequent but marked structure before an infrequent but unmarked structure than vice versa.

Apart from frequency, another confounding factor may be L1 transfer. It has been proposed that learners are much more likely to transfer unmarked structures from their L1 than they are marked structures. Let us consider an example involving pronunciation. English contrasts the sounds /t/ and /d/ word initially (tin/din), word medially (be*tt*ing/be*dd*ing), and word finally (we*t*/we*d*). German, however, only contrasts these two sounds word initially and word medially. Typologically, the word initial contrast is unmarked and the word final contrast marked. It can be predicted, then, that English learners will have no difficulty learning that the word final contrast does not exist in German but that German learners will experience considerable difficulty in learning to make the word final contrast in English. This is what has been found to occur.

Cognitive versus linguistic explanations

In this chapter we have examined a number of ways in which linguistics can assist SLA. The typological study of languages affords interesting predictions about what learners will acquire first and what they will transfer from their L1. UG also serves as a source of finely-tuned hypotheses about what structures will cause learning difficulty and, in addition, raises important questions about whether L2 and L1 acquisition are the same or different.

How should we view these linguistic explanations? Are they alternatives to the psycholinguistic explanations we examined in Chapter 6 or are they complementary? The answer to this depends on whether linguistic universals and markedness are seen as exerting a *direct* effect on L2 acquisition (as is the case in SLA studies based on Chomskyan linguistic theory) or whether they are seen as having only an *indirect* effect, mediated by psycholinguistic mechanisms of the kind considered earlier (a position entirely compatible with the typological study of language). In short, it comes down to whether L2 acquisition is to be explained in terms of a distinct and innate language faculty or in terms of general cognitive abilities. There is no consensus on this issue. It should be noted however that UG does not claim to account for the whole of a language or even the whole of the grammar of a language. As such, it allows for modularity—the existence of different components of language that are learned in different ways, some through UG and others with the assistance of general cognitive abilities.

8
Individual differences in L2 acquisition

So far we have been concerned with describing and explaining the universal aspects of L2 acquisition—the main concern of SLA. However, SLA also acknowledges that there are individual differences in L2 acquisition. We have seen that social factors to do with the context of learning have an effect on how successful individual L2 learners are, and possibly on how interlanguage develops as well. We will now examine a number of psychological dimensions of difference.

These dimensions are many and various. Affective factors such as learners' personalities can influence the degree of anxiety they experience and their preparedness to take risks in learning and using an L2. Learners' preferred ways of learning (their 'learning styles') may influence their overall orientation to the learning task and the kind of input (for example, spoken or written) they find it easiest to work with. We will focus on two of the major dimensions here—language aptitude and motivation—and also explore how differences in learning strategies can affect development.

Language aptitude

It has been suggested that people differ in the extent to which they possess a natural ability for learning an L2. This ability, known as **language aptitude**, is believed to be in part related to general intelligence but also to be in part distinct.

Early work by John Carroll led to the identification of a number of components of language aptitude. These are:

1   Phonemic coding ability, i.e. the ability to identify the sounds of a foreign language so that they can be remembered later. This ability is also seen as related to the ability to handle sound–symbol relationships (for example, to identify the sound which 'th' stands for).

2   Grammatical sensitivity, i.e. the ability to recognize the grammatical functions of words in sentences (for example, the subject and object of a sentence).

3   Inductive language learning ability, i.e. the ability to identify patterns of correspondence and relations between form and meaning (for example, to recognize that in English 'to' can denote direction and 'at' location).

4   Rote learning ability, i.e. the ability to form and remember associations between stimuli. This is believed to be important in vocabulary learning.

Research involving language aptitude has focused on whether and to what extent language aptitude is related to success in L2 learning. There is strong evidence that it is. Learners who score highly on language aptitude tests typically learn rapidly and achieve higher levels of L2 proficiency than learners who obtain low scores. Furthermore, research has shown that this is so whether the measure of L2 proficiency is some kind of formal language test or a measure of more communicative language use.

Most of the research on the relationship between language aptitude and L2 proficiency took place in the 1950s and 1960s and, therefore, predates the birth of SLA. From an SLA perspective the key question is: How does language aptitude relate to the processes of interlanguage development? One interesting possibility is that different components of language aptitude may be implicated in different stages of processing. Phonemic coding ability would seem relevant to the processing of input, grammatical sensitivity and inductive language learning ability to the central processing stages involving interlanguage construction, and memory to the storage and access of language. However, such a proposal, while interesting, remains speculative.

Motivation

Whereas language aptitude concerns the cognitive abilities that underlie successful L2 acquisition, **motivation** involves the attitudes and affective states that influence the degree of effort that learners make to learn an L2. Various kinds of motivation have been identified; **instrumental**, **integrative**, **resultative**, and **intrinsic**.

Instrumental motivation

Learners may make efforts to learn an L2 for some functional reason—to pass an examination, to get a better job, or to get a place at university. In some learning contexts, an instrumental motivation seems to be the major force determining success in L2 learning. For example, in settings where learners are motivated to learn an L2 because it opens up educational and economic opportunities for them.

Integrative motivation

Some learners may choose to learn a particular L2 because they are interested in the people and culture represented by the target-language group. For example, it is this integrative orientation that underlies the motivation that many English speaking Canadians have for learning French. However, in other learning contexts, an integrative motivation does not seem to be so important. In fact, in one study, it was found that less integratively oriented Mexican women in California were more successful in learning English than those who were more integratively oriented. This led the researchers who carried out this study to suggest that some learners may be influenced by a 'Machiavellian motivation'—the desire to learn the L2 in order to manipulate and overcome the people of the target language. Such a view is compatible with Peirce's ideas about the role of social identity in L2 learning (see page 41).

Resultative motivation

An assumption of the research referred to above is that motivation is the *cause* of L2 achievement. However, it is also possible that motivation is the *result* of learning. That is, learners who experience success in learning may become more, or in some contexts, less motivated to learn. This helps to explain the conflicting research results. In a context like Canada, success in learning French may intensify English-speaking learners' liking for French culture. However, in California success in learning English may bring Mexican women into situations where they experience discrimination and thus reduce their appreciation of American culture.

Intrinsic motivation

In some learning situations, it may not be learners' general reasons for learning an L2 that are crucial in determining their motivation. Indeed, it is possible that many learners do not hold distinct attitudes, positive or negative, towards the target-language group. Such is probably the case with many *foreign* language learners. It does not follow, however, that such learners are unmotivated. They may find the kinds of learning tasks they are asked to do intrinsically motivating. According to this view, motivation involves the arousal and maintenance of curiosity and can ebb and flow as a result of such factors as learners' particular interests and the extent to which they feel personally involved in learning activities.

Motivation is clearly a highly complex phenomenon. These four types of motivation should be seen as complementary rather than as distinct and oppositional. Learners can be both integratively and instrumentally motivated at one and the same time. Motivation can result from learning as well as cause it. Furthermore, motivation is dynamic in nature; it is not something that a learner has or does not have but rather something that varies from one moment to the next depending on the learning context or task.

Learning strategies

Language aptitude and motivation constitute general factors that influence the rate and level of L2 achievement. But how does their influence operate? One possibility is that they affect the nature and the frequency with which individual learners use learning strategies.

Learning strategies are the particular approaches or techniques that learners employ to try to learn an L2. They can be behavioural (for example, repeating new words aloud to help you remember them) or they can be mental (for example, using the linguistic or situational context to infer the meaning of a new word). They are typically problem-oriented. That is, learners employ learning strategies when they are faced with some problem, such as how to remember a new word. Learners are generally aware of the strategies they use and, when asked, can explain what they did to try to learn something.

Different kinds of learning strategies have been identified. Cognitive strategies are those that are involved in the analysis, synthesis, or transformation of learning materials. An example is 'recombination', which involves constructing a meaningful sentence by recombining known elements of the L2 in a new way. Metacognitive strategies are those involved in planning, monitoring, and evaluating learning. An example is 'selective attention', where the learner makes a conscious decision to attend to particular aspects of the input. Social/affective strategies concern the ways in which learners choose to interact with other speakers. An example is 'questioning for clarification' (i.e. asking for repetition, a paraphrase, or an example).

There have been various attempts to discover which strategies are important for L2 acquisition. One way is to investigate how 'good language learners' try to learn. This involves identifying learners who have been successful in learning an L2 and interviewing them to find out the strategies that worked for them. One of the main findings of such studies is that successful language learners pay attention to both form and meaning. Good language learners are also very active (i.e. they use strategies for taking charge of their own learning), show awareness of the learning process and their own personal learning styles and, above all, are flexible and appropriate in their use of learning strategies. They seem to be especially adept at using metacognitive strategies.

Other studies have sought to relate learners' reported use of different strategies to their L2 proficiency to try to find out which strategies are important for language development. Such studies have shown, not surprisingly, that successful learners use more strategies than unsuccessful learners. They have also shown that different strategies are related to different aspects of L2 learning.

Thus, strategies that involve formal practice (for example, rehearsing a new word) contribute to the development of linguistic competence whereas strategies involving functional practice (for example, seeking out native speakers to talk to) aid the development of communicative skills. Successful learners may also call on different strategies at different stages of their development. However, there is the problem with how to interpret this research. Does strategy use result in learning or does learning increase learners' ability to employ more strategies? At the moment, it is not clear.

An obvious question concerns how these learning strategies relate to the general kinds of psycholinguistic processes discussed in Chapter 6. What strategies are involved in noticing or noticing the gap, for example? Unfortunately, however, no attempt has yet been made to incorporate the various learning strategies that have been identified into a model of psycholinguistic processing. The approach to date has been simply to describe strategies and quantify their use.

The study of learning strategies is of potential value to language teachers. If those strategies that are crucial for learning can be identified, it may prove possible to train students to use them. We will examine this idea in the broader context of a discussion of the role of instruction in L2 acquisition.

9
Instruction and L2 acquisition

One of the goals of SLA is to improve language teaching. To this end some researchers have studied what impact teaching has on L2 learning. In this chapter we will consider three branches of this research. The first concerns whether teaching learners grammar has any effect on their interlanguage development. Do learners learn the structures they are taught? The second draws on the research into individual learner differences. Do learners learn better if the kind of instruction they receive matches their preferred ways of learning an L2? The third branch looks at strategy training. Does it help to teach learners how to use the learning strategies employed by 'good language learners'? In each case, we will consider the main issues involved and sample some of the studies that have been carried out.

Form-focused instruction

Traditionally, language pedagogy has emphasized form-focused instruction. The Grammar Translation Method and the Audiolingual Method both involve attempts to teach learners grammar, differing only in how this is to be accomplished. More recently, however, language pedagogy has emphasized the need to provide learners with real communicative experiences. Communicative Language Teaching is premised on the assumption that learners do not need to be taught grammar before they can communicate but will acquire it naturally as part of the process of learning to communicate. In some versions of Communicative Language Teaching, then, there is no place at all for the direct teaching of grammar.

This brief review of the pedagogical background suggests that there are two key questions: (1) Does form-focused instruction work (i.e. do learners learn what they have been taught)? and, assuming a positive answer to (1), (2) What kind of form-focused instruction works best?

Does form-focused instruction work?

One way in which we might investigate whether formal instruction has any effect on interlanguage is to compare the development of untutored and tutored learners. If we find no differences in the order and sequence of L2 acquisition this would suggest that form-focused instruction has no effect. On the other hand, the existence of differences would suggest that form-focused instruction does have an impact.

In one such study, Teresa Pica compared three groups of L2 learners—an untutored group, a tutored group, and a mixed group (i.e. one that had experienced both instruction and naturalistic learning). She found that the accuracy order of a number of grammatical features (see page 21) was broadly the same in the three groups, suggesting that instruction had had little overall effect on acquisition. However, when she looked closely at particular features she found some interesting differences in them. The tutored group was more accurate on plural *-s* than the untutored group but less accurate on progressive verb *-ing*. The mixed group was intermediate in both cases. In contrast, there were no accuracy differences among the three groups on articles. These results led Pica to suggest that the effects of instruction may depend on the target structure that is being taught. If the structure is formally simple and manifests a straightforward form–function relationship (as in the case of plural *-s*) instruction may lead to improved accuracy. If the structure is formally simple and salient but is functionally fairly complex (as is the case with progressive *-ing*) instruction may help learners to learn the form but not its use so learners end up making a lot of errors. If a structure lacks saliency and is functionally very complex (as is the case with English articles) instruction has no effect at all.

The question is how significant the effects of instruction actually are. Only if the instruction can be shown to enable learners to construct 'rules' can it be said to have an effect on the their underlying competence. The distinction between item learning and system learning (see page 13) is important here. When learners are taught the French articles 'le' and 'la' they may succeed in learning which article to use with the specific set of nouns that were the focus of the instruction. That is, they learn the gender of each noun as a separate item. However, they may fail to develop an understanding of the complex rules that account for whether a noun is masculine or feminine in French. Instruction, then, may be effective in teaching items but not in teaching systems, particularly when these are complex.

There are, in fact, strong theoretical grounds for believing that instruction will not have any long-lasting effect on the way in which learners construct their interlanguage systems. In Chapter 2 we saw that learners appear to possess some kind of 'built-in syllabus' that regulates how and when they acquire particular grammatical structures. It is possible that this 'syllabus' is not amenable to modification from the outside.

This claim can be tested by investigating whether instruction has any effect on the sequence of acquisition of particular grammatical structures. Again, one way of doing this is by comparing tutored and untutored learners. In one such study, a comparison was made between the acquisition of German word-order rules by a group of adult classroom learners and that reported for migrant workers acquiring German without instruction in Germany (see page 58). The sequence was the same, suggesting that the instruction had had no effect on the processing strategies involved in the acquisition of these word-order rules. The instructed learners seemed to follow their own syllabus. However, they proceeded through this syllabus more rapidly than the untutored learners and were more likely to reach the final stage.

Another way of testing the claim is by designing instructional experiments to see if teaching a particular structure results in its acquisition. There have been a number of such experiments. Manfred Pienemann, for example, investigated whether form-focused instruction led to a group of ten-year-old children acquiring one of the German word-order rules (the inversion rule). He reports in detail on only two of the children but the results are highly suggestive. One of the learners, Giovanni, had already reached a stage of development immediately prior to the stage at which the target structure is naturally acquired. In this case, the instruction was effective. Giovanni acquired the inversion rule. The other learner, Teresa, was far less advanced and for her the instruction did not work. She failed to acquire inversion.

This study, together with additional research carried out in Australia, led Pienemann to propose the **teachability hypothesis**. This hypothesis predicts that instruction can only promote language acquisition if the interlanguage is close to the point when the structure to be taught is acquired in the natural setting (so that sufficient processing requirements are developed). So the teachability hypothesis, which has received considerable support in recent research, suggests that instruction does not subvert the natural sequence of acquisition but rather helps to speed up learners' passage through it. The pedagogic relevance of this, however, is limited as teachers are not likely to know which learners in their class are ready to be taught a particular structure and will have no easy way of finding out.

Pienemann's research shows that form-focused instruction can have an effect on acquisition. But how durable are these effects? Early research on progressive -*ing*, for example, revealed that instruction in this feature caused learners to increase their use of it in their communicative speech, often incorrectly, but that the effects were short-lived. Another study, directed at teaching French learners of English that placing an adverb between the verb and the direct object of a sentence is ungrammatical (see page 66), produced similar results. Initial gains in accuracy disappeared over time.

Other studies, however, have shown that instruction can have effects that are both beneficial and long-lasting. For example, a carefully designed set of materials for teaching the distinction between two French verb tenses resulted in clear gains in accuracy, which were evident not only immediately after the period of instruction but also three months later. In fact, the learners' ability to use these verb forms correctly went on improving. There is ample evidence that the acquisition of at least some linguistic structures can be permanently influenced by instruction.

The question arises as to why some structures seem to be permanently affected and others are not? One possibility is that it depends on the nature of the instruction. Another possibility, which we have already examined, is that it depends on the nature of the target structure. For example, when the instruction affects system learning the effects may be long-lasting but when it only influences item learning the effects may be less durable. A third possibility is that long-lasting effects occur only when learners have subsequent opportunities to hear and use the target structure in communication. This might explain why instruction produces durable effects for French verb tenses and for question forms, which occur frequently, but not for adverbs, which do not. However, we do not yet have a definite answer to this important question.

So far we have considered whether learners learn what they have been taught. However, it is clearly not possible to teach learners all the rules of the grammar of a language. There are simply too many. What, though, if teaching learners one grammatical structure triggers acquisition of one or more other structures? This is a distinct possibility given that some grammatical structures seem to be implicated with each other. For example, according to the accessibility hierarchy, the existence of a marked relative pronoun function in a language implicates the existence of other less marked functions. As we have already seen (page 64), this seems to hold true for interlanguages. An intriguing possibility, therefore, is that if learners can discover that the target language permits a marked function they will be able to generalize this knowledge to the unmarked functions. A number of studies have explored this possibility with interesting results. Teaching learners a relatively marked function, such as indirect object, does appear to trigger acquisition of the unmarked direct object and subject functions. However, it is not yet clear if such effects are durable nor is it clear whether this triggering effect applies to other grammatical structures.

Finally, we need to consider exactly what we mean by 'acquisition' when we talk about the effects of instruction. This is a crucial issue. It is one thing for instruction to have an effect on learners' ability to manipulate structures consciously and quite another for it to affect their ability to use structures with ease and accuracy in fluent communication. There is now ample evidence that the effects of form-focused instruction are not restricted to careful language use but are also evident in free communication.

What kind of form-focused instruction works best?

Given that instruction can work, it becomes important to discover whether some kinds of instruction work better than others. Arguably, it is this question that is of greater interest to teachers. The issues at stake are not merely a question of pedagogical efficiency, however. They are also of considerable theoretical significance for SLA.

To illustrate this we will consider a number of options in form-focused instruction. The first concerns the distinction between input-based and production-based practice. Traditionally, grammar teaching has emphasized production. Indeed, language pedagogy offers a rich array of techniques for eliciting the production of targeted structures from students (for example, substitution drills, blank-filling exercises, dialogues, and games of various kinds). However, as we have seen, some theories of SLA see interlanguage as driven by input rather than output. An interesting question—from both a pedagogical and a theoretical standpoint—is whether instruction that emphasizes input-processing (A in Figure 9.1) works better than instruction that emphasizes output production (B in Figure 9.1).

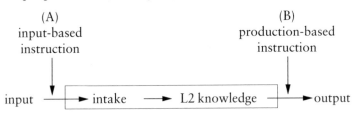

FIGURE 9.1 *Input-based and production-based instruction*

An experimental study carried out by Bill VanPatten and Teresa Cadierno was designed to investigate this. One group of learners was exposed to traditional **production-based instruction**, and another to **input-based instruction** where they had to listen to and respond to sentences containing the target structure. At the end of the instruction both groups completed two tests, one a test of production and the other a test of comprehension. The group that received the input-based instruction did far better on the comprehension test and just as well on the production test. This study, then, suggests that form-focused instruction that emphasizes input processing may be very effective. It also supports theories of L2 acquisition that emphasize the role of conscious noticing in input; input-based instruction may work because it induces noticing in learners.

The second issue, concerns **consciousness-raising**. This term refers to attempts to make learners aware of the existence of specific linguistic features in the target language. One way in which this can be done is by supplying the learner with positive evidence. An alternative approach is to provide negative evidence.

In Chapter 7 we saw that children rely more or less exclusively on positive evidence. The fact that such evidence fails to supply the information children need to master their L1 constitutes a major argument in support of the existence of UG. The issue in SLA is whether adult L2 learners can also learn from positive evidence or whether they require negative evidence, at least for some structures. This addresses the wider issue of whether older learners have continued access to UG (see page 69). If adult L2 learners can learn solely from positive input this would suggest that UG is still available to them; conversely, if they cannot, this is an indication that it is not available.

To test whether positive input is sufficient, Martha Trahey and Lydia White designed a study in which eleven-year-old French learners of L2 English were given instruction where they were 'flooded' with input containing adverb sentences over a two-week period. The children were not given any explicit information about adverb sentences or any negative feedback (i.e. they were not corrected). In one respect, the positive evidence worked. The learners showed a dramatic increase in the use of subject–adverb–verb–object (SAVO) sentences, for example:

Anne quietly watched the television.

In another respect, however, it did not work, as the learners continued to make errors by inserting the adverb between the verb and direct object (SVAO), as in:

Anne watched quietly the television.

This suggests that positive evidence is not sufficient to reset a parameter and, perhaps, that UG is not available to L2 learners of this age. It is possible, of course, that more positive input would have done the job. The implication for language pedagogy is that positive input in the form of **input flooding** may help learners to start using some difficult forms (like SAVO) but may not be sufficient to destabilize interlanguage and prevent fossilization. That is, positive input does not show learners that forms like SVAO are ungrammatical.

If positive evidence does not work, then, perhaps negative evidence does. Another study by White, referred to earlier, found that giving learners explicit information about adverb sentences together with negative feedback did enable them, temporarily at least, to reduce instances of the SVAO error. Other studies have also shown that learners are able to make use of negative evidence, in the form of teacher correction, to eliminate errors in their production.

The task of teasing out how the various instructional options affect the acquisition of grammatical structures has only just begun. The promise of such studies is that they can make a contribution to both language pedagogy, by helping to make teaching more efficient, and to SLA, by providing a means of testing theories of acquisition.

Learner–instruction matching

A distinct possibility, however, is that the same instructional option is not equally effective for all L2 learners. Individual differences to do with such factors as learning style and language aptitude are likely to influence which options work best.

For example, the type of instruction learners can benefit from most may depend on the nature of their language aptitude (see page 73). Learners vary in the particular types of ability they are strong in. Some learners are good at segmenting sounds in the speech they hear but are less effective at identifying the grammatical functions of words in sentences. Other learners are the opposite. Learners with differing kinds of ability may be able to achieve similar levels of success providing that the type of instruction enables them to maximize their strengths. There is some evidence to suggest that this is the case.

It is obviously important to take individual differences into account when investigating the effects of instruction. For example, even if it is eventually shown that input-based instruction works better overall than production-based instruction, it does not follow that this will be true for all learners.

Strategy training

Teaching learners specific grammatical structures constitutes an attempt to intervene directly in interlanguage development. An alternative approach is to intervene more indirectly by identifying strategies that are likely to promote acquisition and providing training in them.

Most of the research on strategy training has focused on vocabulary learning. The results have been rather mixed. Training students to use strategies that involve different ways of making associations involving target words has generally proved successful. For example, the key word method requires learners to form two kinds of associations. First, learners associate the target word with a word which is the same or similar to an L1 word (for example, the Japanese word 'ohio', meaning 'morning', might be associated with 'Ohio', a state in the United States). Second, the L1 word is linked to a mental image that incorporates the meaning of the target word (for example, the learner thinks of a very cold morning in winter in Ohio). These associations have been shown to promote both retention of and access to the target word. However, other studies have been less convincing in demonstrating the effectiveness of strategy training.

The idea of strategy training is attractive because it provides a way of helping learners to become autonomous (i.e. of enabling them to take responsibility for their own learning). The main problem is that not enough is known about which strategies and which combinations of strategies work best for L2 acquisition.

Summary

In this section we have examined whether it is possible to teach an L2. We have seen that direct instruction can help in a number of ways. It can lead to enhanced accuracy, it can help learners progress through developmental stages more rapidly, and it can destabilize interlanguage grammars that have fossilized. However, direct instruction is not always successful nor are its effects always durable. Constraining factors are the nature of the target structure and the learner's stage of development. Less is currently known about what type of direct instruction works best. Input-based instruction may prove as effective as production-based instruction and, perhaps, even more so. Input-flooding may help students learn features in the input but does not destabilize interlanguage grammars (i.e. it does not get rid of established errors). For this, explicit instruction and negative feedback may be needed. It is also very likely that the effectiveness of different types of instruction will depend on the abilities and predispositions of individual learners. An alternative to direct instruction is strategy training. However, uncertainty exists regarding the content, methodology, and outcomes of such training.

10
Conclusion: multiple perspectives in SLA

It is tempting to try to conclude this brief survey of SLA by offering a general model of L2 acquisition that incorporates all the various perspectives we have explored. However, there is a good reason for not doing this; there is no single theory or model or even framework that can adequately incorporate the range of hypotheses which SLA has addressed. To put it another way, there is no single metaphor that can encompass all the metaphors that SLA has drawn on to explain how learners acquire an L2. What single theory can adequately encompass such disparate metaphors as 'investment', 'social distance', 'accommodation', 'scaffolding', 'noticing', 'interfacing', 'fossilization', 'monitoring', 'avoidance', 'Machiavellian motivation', 'intervention', and so on? It is true, as we have seen, that there is a dominant metaphor in SLA—that of the computer—but this excludes as much as it includes and, dangerously, forces a particular interpretation of what is involved in L2 acquisition on the reader.

There is, however, considerable disagreement within SLA about the need for a single model or, at least, the need for some principled selection among the theoretical positions on offer. On the one hand, there are those who argue that SLA needs to engage in the careful elimination of theories to demonstrate its maturity as a discipline. On the other hand, there are those who argue that L2 acquisition is a highly complex phenomenon and that, therefore, multiple theories are both inevitable and desirable. These different positions about the role of theory in SLA also call upon different metaphors; we can 'cull' theories or we can 'let all the flowers grow'.

The types of enquiry that characterize SLA and the types of

explanations provided reflect the different purposes of researchers. Some researchers have been primarily concerned with language pedagogy and have seen SLA as contributing to more effective language teaching. Others have been more concerned with linguistics and have seen SLA as a way of testing hypotheses about the nature of language. Still others have been concerned with the sociology of multilingual communities and are interested in SLA because it serves to illustrate how social context affects and is affected by language. For this reason alone we are likely to see SLA continue to offer multiple perspectives.

SECTION 2
Readings

Chapter 1
Introduction: describing and explaining L2 acquisition

Text 1

RICHARD SCHMIDT: 'Interaction, acculturation and the acquisition of communicative competence: a case study of an adult' in N. Wolfson and E. Judd (eds.): *Sociolinguistics and Second Language Acquisition*. Newbury House 1983, pages 168–9

In the following text, Schmidt asks to what extent Wes, the subject of his case study, is a 'good language learner'. He concludes that there is no straightforward answer to this question, that it depends on what is meant by 'language'.

Whether one considers Wes to be a good language learner or a poor language learner depends very much on one's definition of language and of the content of SLA. If language is seen as a means of initiating, maintaining, and regulating relationships and carrying on the business of living, then perhaps Wes is a good learner. If one views language as a system of elements and rules, with syntax playing a major role, then Wes is clearly a very poor learner. Friends and acquaintances who are not in the language or language teaching business generally evaluate Wes's English favorably, pointing out, for example, that 'I understand him a lot better than X, who's been here over twenty years.' Several sociolinguists with whom I have discussed his case have given similar evaluations, sometimes proclaiming him a superior language learner who just doesn't care about grammatical do-dads, most of which are eliminated in normal speech anyway. Grammar teachers, on the other hand, generally consider him a disaster, possibly beyond rescue. Wes's own evaluation of his English ability is mixed, recognizing both strengths and weaknesses. He is quite clearly proud of what he has accomplished and knows that he can communicate much better in English than many nonnative speakers with much greater linguistic knowledge. ...

▷ *In what respects is Wes a 'good language learner' and in what respects is he not one?*

▷ *What is your own definition of a 'good language learner'?*

Schmidt now goes on to consider why Wes failed to learn the grammar of English. He examines a number of possible explanations, social and individual, but dismisses them all.

... It seems to me quite clear that Wes's failure to learn much of the grammatical component of his second language cannot be attributed to SOCIAL DISTANCE factors, to lack of need for or interest in meaningful communication and interaction, to personality factors such as self-consciousness, or to poor attitudes toward target language speakers. Low social distance, positive attitudes toward the second language community, and high integrative motivation to use the second language for communication have led to a considerable increase in overall *communicative* competence but have had little effect on improved *grammatical* competence.

▷ *What explanation can you offer for Wes's failure to acquire grammatical competence in English?*

Text 2
ROD ELLIS: 'Learning to communicate in the classroom: a study of two language learners' requests' in *Studies in Second Language Acquisition* 14, 1992, pages 20–21

Whereas Wes learned English in a natural context, the two learners discussed in the following text learned in a classroom context. Like Wes they were in some respects successful but their development was limited.

The classroom context in which J and R learned English afforded ample opportunities for natural language use. It enabled J and R to develop a basic ability to perform requests using target language forms. In addition, it proved sufficient to motivate the acquisition of a variety of linguistic exponents for encoding requests, thus affording the learners some degree of choice in the realization of their requests. ...

However, the study also found that J and R failed to acquire a full range of request types and forms. It also showed that they developed only a limited ability to vary their choice of request strategy in accordance with situational factors. One explanation for this is that the developmental process was not complete. However, it may be that even with more time the classroom environment is insufficient to guarantee the development of full target language norms, possibly because the kind of 'communicative need' that the learners experienced was insufficient to ensure development of the full range of request types and strategies. ... J and R had a clear interpersonal need to learn how to perform requests, and they also appeared to experience an expressive need to vary the way in which they performed them. It is less certain, however, that in the classroom situation they found themselves in they recognized any definite sociolinguistic need.

▷ *In what respects were J and R successful in learning how to make requests and in what respects were they unsuccessful?*

▷ *What do you think Ellis means by 'interpersonal need', 'expressive need', and 'sociolinguistic need'?*

▷ *How convincing do you find Ellis's explanations for the learners' lack of success? What other explanations might there be?*

Chapter 2
The nature of learner language

Errors and error analysis

Text 3
S. PIT CORDER: 'The significance of learners' errors' in *International Review of Applied Linguistics* 5. Also in *Error*

Analysis and Interlanguage. Oxford University Press 1981, page 10

One of the problems in describing learner language is that learners are not alone in producing deviant language; native speakers sometimes do so as well. This raises the important question as to how we can distinguish the deviations of learners from those of native speakers.

... The opposition between systematic and non-systematic errors is important. We are all aware that in normal adult speech in our native language we are continually committing errors of one sort or another. These, as we have so often been reminded recently, are due to memory lapses, physical states such as tiredness, and psychological conditions such as strong emotion. These are adventitious artefacts of linguistic performance and do not reflect a defect in our knowledge of our own language. We are normally immediately aware of them when they occur and can correct them with more or less complete assurance. It would be quite unreasonable to expect the learner of a second language not to exhibit such slips of the tongue (or pen), since he is subject to similar external and internal conditions when performing in his first or second language. We must therefore make a distinction between those errors which are the product of such chance circumstances and those which reveal his underlying knowledge of the language to date, or, as we may call it his *transitional competence.* The errors of performance will characteristically be unsystematic and the errors of competence, systematic. ... It will be useful therefore hereafter to refer to errors of performance as *mistakes*, reserving the term *error* to refer to the systematic errors of the learner from which we are able to reconstruct his knowledge of the language to date, i.e. his *transitional competence.*

▷ *What does Corder mean by saying that an 'error' is 'systematic' and a 'mistake' is 'unsystematic'? Do you see any problems with this definition?*

▷ *Later Corder recognizes that it may be difficult to distinguish 'errors' and 'mistakes'. Can you suggest ways of doing this?*

Developmental patterns

Text 4

HERLINDA CANCINO, ELLEN ROSANSKY, and JOHN SCHUMANN: 'The acquisition of English negatives and interrogatives by native Spanish speakers' in E. Hatch (ed.): *Second Language Acquisition*. Newbury House 1978, pages 209–11

This text outlines the method of analysis used to identify the sequence of acquisition for negatives which six native speakers of Spanish (two young children, two adolescents, and two adults) manifested over a ten-month period.

We did, however, think that perhaps traditional grammatical descriptions in the form of rules could be made of such linguistic subsystems as negative, interrogative or auxiliary. Our attempts to write rules for the negative proved fruitless. The constant development and concomitant variation in our subjects' speech at any one point made the task impossible. The technique to which we turned was to catalogue the various negating devices (*no*, *don't*, *can't*, *isn't*, etc.) and for each sample to determine the proportion of each negating device to total number of negatives (including negated adjectives, nouns adverbs, etc.) used by our subjects. ...

For all subjects, we have eliminated the expression 'I don't know', which seemed to be a memorized whole (or, using Evelyn Hatch's term, a 'routine formula'). ...

▷ *What do Cancino et al. mean by 'rules'? Can you state the rules for verb negation in English?*

▷ *Why exactly did they abandon the attempt to write rules for the six learners?*

▷ *Why was it important to eliminate routine formulas from the analysis?*

And here is the sequence of acquisition that was identified.

The 'cataloguing' approach produced the following results:

1 The subjects began negating by using *no* V constructions.
   Marta: I no can see.
               Carolina no go to play. ...

2 At the same time or shortly after the *no V* constructions appear, the subjects begin to negate using *don't V* constructions. Examples of *don't V* utterances are:

Marta: I don't hear.
He don't like it. ...

3 Next the subjects used the *aux-neg* constructions in which the negative is placed after the auxiliary. In general the first auxiliaries to be negated in this way were *is* and *can*.

Marta: Somebody is not coming in.
You can't tell her. ...

4 Finally, they learned the analyzed forms of *don't* (do not, doesn't, does not, didn't, did not):

Marta: It doesn't spin.
One night I didn't have the light.

▷ *Cancino et al. offer two possible reasons for why the learners began with 'no + verb' constructions. What are they? How could you decide which of these explanations is correct?*

▷ *Explain how the 'don't + V' stage differs from the 'aux + neg' stage.*

▷ *Why do you think 'analyzed don't' is the last stage in the sequence?*

Variability in learner language

The two texts here contrast two views about the significance of variability in learner language. Gregg sees competence as homogeneous and treats variability as an aspect of performance. Tarone sees the learner's competence itself as variable.

Text 5

KEVIN GREGG: 'The variable competence model of second language acquisition and why it isn't' in *Applied Linguistics* 11, 1990, pages 364 and 369

One of the incontrovertible facts of language use, whether L1 or L2, is that it varies. It varies across members of a speech community (I say tomayto, you say tomahto); it varies for the output of any given acquirer of a language, whether over time

(I say tomayto, I used to say tomahto) or at any given time (I say tomayto, but I also say tomahto). The fact is incontrovertible; is it interesting? Or rather—since of course nothing human is alien to us, etc., and there's no disputing, etc.—is this fact of importance in constructing a theory of second language acquisition? Is it a fact to be dealt with by a theory, or is it simply that least valued of objects in scientific enquiry, a mere fact? Do we extend our investigation to the question of who says potayto and who says potahto, or do we call the whole thing off? ...

... It is not self-evident that systematicity should be a sufficient condition for calling something part of competence. Nor is it clear in what way performance ('learner behaviour'), systematic or otherwise, can be regarded as part of competence. This merging of performance and competence robs the concept of competence, under whatever name, of any useful function.

▷ *How would Gregg view the various types of variability in learner language discussed in the Survey? Why would he view them in this way?*

Text 6

ELAINE TARONE: 'On variation in interlanguage: a response to Gregg' in *Applied Linguistics* 11, 1990, page 394

... First, let us look at a variationist view of what gets acquired. In this view, knowledge itself can be variable, not always categorical. It is not the case that you *always* either know the rule or you don't. Especially when it is in the process of being formed, knowledge itself may be partial, fuzzy, or contain conflicting elements, as Romaine (1984) points out:

Rule acquisition is not an all or nothing affair, and presumably 'complete' mastery involves both comprehension and production. There may be a number of aspects of the internal workings of a rule, some of which may be acquired before others. There are social dimensions of a rule relating to its use. (Romaine 1984: 78–9)

If we view knowledge itself as containing variability, the competence/performance distinction may become unnecessary.

▷ *In what ways do Tarone's views about variability differ from Gregg's?*

▷ *From your reading about variability in learner language in the Survey section, which of these positions (Gregg's or Tarone's) do you favour and why?*

Chapter 3
Interlanguage

Text 7

S. PIT CORDER: 'Language continua and the interlanguage hypothesis' in Proceedings of the Fifth Neuchâtel Colloquium, 1977. Also in *Error Analysis and Interlanguage*. Oxford University Press 1981, pages 87–8

According to interlanguage theory, L2 acquisition entails a continuum of evolving systems. A key issue, then, is what this continuum consists of. Here Corder outlines one view— not his own.

Although it is nowhere explicitly stated in his paper, it is evident that Selinker conceived of interlanguage as a 'dynamic system'. … He makes it clear that he regards the 'interlanguage system' as the product of a psycholinguistic process of interaction between two linguistic systems, those of the mother tongue and the target language. He furthermore expounds at considerable length the notion of 'fossilization' which he characterizes as a 'mechanism' whereby 'speakers of a particular native language will keep certain linguistic items, rules, subsystems in their interlanguage, no matter what amount of instruction they receive in the target language'. Selinker therefore clearly conceived of interlanguage as being a *continuum*. …

What is, with hindsight, strikingly absent in Selinker's original formulation is the notion of the interlanguage continuum as having the property of increasing complexity or elaboration. There is nothing in his original article which suggests that he saw the interlanguage continuum as anything but a *restructuring* of the learner's system from native language to target language *at the same level of complexity*. …

So long as the concept of an interlanguage continuum was one of restructuring alone, it was bound to remain of relatively little value or generality, since it could only be seen as movement between one fully complex code and another. There were, therefore, as many interlanguage continua as there were languages involved in the learning situation and the sequences of restructuring would all be different and the errors predicted by the theory would all be 'transfer' errors.

▷ What is meant by describing the interlanguage continuum as a 'restructuring continuum'?

▷ What objections can be levelled against this view of the interlanguage continuum?

▷ In what other ways might the interlanguage continuum be characterized?

Chapter 4
Social aspects of interlanguage

Text 8

JOHN SCHUMANN: *The Pidginization Process: a Model for Second Language Acquisition*. Newbury House 1978, pages 80–1

Here Schumann describes two kinds of bad learning situations based on the factors contributing to social distance. (TL = target language; 2LL = second language learner.)

One of the bad situations ... would be where the TL group views the 2LL group as dominant and the 2LL group views itself in the same way; where both groups desire preservation and high enclosure for the 2LL group; where the 2LL group is both cohesive and large; where the two cultures are not congruent; where the two groups hold negative attitudes toward each other, and where the 2LL group intends to remain in the TL area for only a short time. This type of situation is likely to develop for Americans living in Riyadh, Saudi Arabia. ...

The second bad situation ... has all the characteristics of the first except that in this case the 2LL group would consider itself subordinate and would also be considered subordinate by the TL group. This has been the traditional situation of Navajo Indians living in the Southwest, and of American Indians in general.

▷ *Which of these two bad learning situations applies to Alberto, the Costa Rican immigrant worker Schumann studied?*

▷ *Can you think of any other examples of these two bad learning situations?*

▷ *Can you think of any exceptions (i.e. 2LL groups who are in bad learning situations but who are successful)? What explanation can you give for these exceptions?*

▷ *Can you think of examples of good learning situations?*

Text 9

BONNY N. PEIRCE: 'Social identity, investment, and language learning' in *TESOL Quarterly* 29, 1995, pages 15–16

Here Peirce describes some of the theoretical thinking that informed her study of the acquisition of English by adult women immigrants in Canada.

... Whereas humanist conceptions of the individual—and most definitions of the individual in SLA research—presuppose that every person has an essential, unique, fixed, and coherent core (introvert/extrovert; motivated/unmotivated; field dependent/field independent), poststructuralism depicts the individual as diverse, contradictory, and dynamic; multiple rather than unitary, decentered rather than centered. ...

... the conception of social identity as a site of struggle is an extension of the position that social identity is multiple and contradictory. Subjectivity is produced in a variety of social sites, all of which are structured by relations of power in which the person takes up different subject positions—teacher, mother, manager, critic—some positions of which may be in conflict with others. In addition, the subject is not conceived of as passive; he/she is conceived of as both subject of and subject to relations of power within a particular site, community, and society: The subject has human agency. Thus the subject positions that a person takes up within a particular discourse are open to argument:

Although a person may be positioned in a particular way within a given discourse, the person might resist the subject position or even set up a counterdiscourse which positions the person in a powerful rather than marginalized subject position.

▷ *Can you think of some of the 'multiple identities' that might characterize the lives of immigrant learners of English in countries like Canada?*

▷ *What kinds of identity are likely to promote their L2 learning?*

▷ *How do you think Peirce would explain Alberto's failure to acquire much English?*

Chapter 5
Discourse aspects of interlanguage

Text 10

STEPHEN KRASHEN: *The Input Hypothesis: Issues and Implications.* Longman, 1985, pages 2–3

In this text, Krashen argues that acquisition will take place automatically if learners receive 'comprehensible input'. Krashen's views have had a notable impact on SLA and also on language pedagogy.

The Input Hypothesis claims that humans acquire language in only one way—by understanding messages, or by receiving 'comprehensible input'. We progress along the natural order ... by understanding input that contains structures at our next 'stage'— structures that are a bit beyond our current level of competence. (We move from i, our current level, to $i + 1$, the next level along the natural order, by understanding input containing $i + 1$; ...). We are able to understand language containing unacquired grammar with the help of context, which includes extra-linguistic information, our knowledge of the world, and previously acquired linguistic competence. The caretaker provides extra-linguistic context by limiting speech to the child to the 'here and now'. The beginning-language teacher provides context via visual aids (pictures and objects) and discussion of familiar topics. The Input Hypothesis has two corollaries:

a Speaking is a result of acquisition and not its cause. Speech cannot be taught directly but 'emerges' on its own as a result of building competence via comprehensible input.

b If input is understood, and there is enough of it, the necessary grammar is automatically provided. The language teacher need not attempt deliberately to teach the next structure along the natural order—it will be provided in just the right quantities and automatically reviewed if the student receives a sufficient amount of comprehensible input.

To be more precise, input is the essential environmental ingredient. The acquirer does not simply acquire what he hears—there is a significant contribution of the internal language processor (Chomsky's Language Acquisition Device: LAD). Not all the input the acquirer hears is processed for acquisition, and the LAD itself generates possible rules according to innate procedures. ... Moreover, not all comprehended input reaches the LAD. ...

▷ *To what extent is Krashen's Input Hypothesis a mentalist theory?*

▷ *Krashen offers no explanation here (or elsewhere) of the process by which comprehending input results in 'intake'. Can you provide one?*

▷ *It has been pointed out that if learners can comprehend input easily there is no reason for them to learn any new language from it and that it is, in fact, input that they do not understand that is important for acquisition. How might 'incomprehensible input' lead to acquisition?*

▷ *'Speaking is the result of acquisition and not its cause.' Do you agree? What counter arguments can you think of?*

Text 11

MICHAEL LONG: 'Native speaker/non-native speaker conversation in the second-language classroom' in M. Clarke and J. Handscombe (eds.): *On TESOL '82*. TESOL 1983, pages 211–12

Like Krashen, Long views comprehensible input as the source of acquisition. However, he differs from Krashen in emphasizing one particular way of achieving comprehensible input—meaning negotiation.

... there is a logical problem with the idea that changing the input will aid *acquisition*. If removal from the input of structures and lexical items the learner does not understand is what is involved in making speech comprehensible, how does the learner ever advance? Where is the input at the i + 1 that is to appear in the learner's competence at the next stage of development?

Clearly, there must be other ways in which input is made comprehensible than modifying the input itself. One way, as Krashen, Hatch and others have argued, is by use of the linguistic and extralinguistic context to fill in the gaps, just as NSs have been shown to do when the incoming speech signal is inadequate ... . Another way, as in caretaker speech, is through orienting even adult-adult NS-NNS conversation to the 'here and now' ... . A third, more consistently used method is modifying not the input itself, but the *interactional structure of conversation* through such devices as self- and other-repetition, confirmation and comprehension checks and clarification requests. ...

Two pieces of evidence suggest that this third way of making input comprehensible is the most important and most widely used of all. First, all studies which have looked at this dimension of NS-NNS conversation have found statistically significant modifications from NS-NS norms. Interactional modifications, in other words, are pervasive. Second, interactional modifications are found in NS-NNS conversation even when input modifications are not or are few and minor.

▷ *Why does Long claim that simplified input (of the kind found in foreigner talk) does not assist acquisition? What evidence does he give to support this claim? Can you think of any counter arguments?*

▷ *Can you construct a brief example of NS–NNS conversation to illustrate how the interactional structure of a conversation is modified using one of the devices (for example, confirmation checks) that Long mentions?*

▷ Long suggests that both a 'here and now' orientation in con- versation and modifying the interactional structure assist acquisition, but he clearly favours the latter. Why do you think this is?

Text 12

MERRILL SWAIN: 'Three functions of output in second language learning' in G. Cook and B. Seidlhofer (eds.): *Principle and Practice in Applied Linguistics*. Oxford University Press 1995, pages 125–6

Whereas Krashen sees no role for speaking in L2 acquisition, other researchers, such as Merrill Swain, consider learner output an important mechanism of acquisition.

… the output hypothesis claims that producing language serves second language acquisition in several ways. One function of producing the target language, in the sense of 'practising', is that it enhances fluency. This seems non-controversial, particularly if it is not confused with the adage that 'practice makes perfect'. We know that fluency and accuracy are different dimensions of language performance, and although practice may enhance fluency, it does not necessarily improve accuracy (Ellis 1988; Schmidt 1992).

Other functions of output in second language acquisition have been proposed that relate more to accuracy and fluency. … First, it is hypothesized that output promotes 'noticing'. That is to say, in producing the target language (vocally or subvocally) learners may notice a gap between what they *want* to say and what they *can* say, leading them to recognize what they do not know, or know only partially. In other words, under some circumstances, the activity of producing the target language may prompt second language learners to consciously recognize some of their linguistic problems; it may bring to their attention something they need to discover about their L2 (Swain 1993). This may trigger cognitive processes which might generate linguistic knowledge that is new for learners, or which consolidate their existing knowledge (Swain and Lapkin 1994).

A second way in which producing language may serve the language learning process is through hypothesis testing. That is, producing output is one way of testing a hypothesis about comprehensibility or linguistic well-formedness. A considerable body of research and theorizing over the last two decades has suggested that output, particularly erroneous output, can often be an indication that a learner has formulated a hypothesis about how the language works, and is testing it out. ... Sometimes this output invokes feedback which can lead learners to modify or 'reprocess' their output.

Thirdly, as learners reflect upon their own target language use, their output serves a metalinguistic function, enabling them to control and internalize linguistic knowledge. My assumption at present is that there is theoretical justification for considering a distinct metalinguistic function of output.

▷ *Swain distinguishes the effects of output on 'fluency' and 'accuracy'. What exactly does she mean by these terms and why is this distinction important in considering the role of output?*

▷ *Think of concrete examples to illustrate the three functions of output that Swain proposes.*

▷ *What arguments might Krashen use to combat Swain's claims regarding the role of output in L2 acquisition?*

Text 13

RICHARD DONATO: 'Collective scaffolding in second language learning' in J. Lantolf and G. Appel (eds.): *Vygotskian Approaches to Second Language Research.* Ablex 1994, pages 44–5

Donato documents ways in which learners talking among themselves are able to 'scaffold' knowledge which beforehand none of them possessed. His research draws on Vygotsky's ideas about the role of interpersonal interaction in learning (see page 48 in the Survey).

A1 Speaker 1 ... and then I'll say ... *tu as souvenu notre anniversaire de marriage* ... or should I say *mon anniversaire?*
A2 Speaker 2 *Tu as ...*
A3 Speaker 3 *Tu as ...*

A4	Speaker 1	*Tu as souvenu* … 'you remembered?'
A5	Speaker 3	Yea, but isn't that reflexive? *Tu t'as* …
A6	Speaker 1	Ah, *tu t'as souvenu.*
A7	Speaker 2	Oh, it's *tu es*
A8	Speaker 1	*Tu es*
A9	Speaker 3	*tu es, tu es, tu* …
A10	Speaker 1	*T'es, tu t'es*
A11	Speaker 3	*tu t'es*
A12	Speaker 1	*Tu t'es souvenu.*

Protocol A is an attempt to render 'you remembered' into French. The compound past tense formation of reflective [*sic*] verbs in French presents complex linguistic processing, since students are required to choose the auxiliary *être* instead of *avoir*, select the correct reflexive pronoun to agree with the subject, form the past participle, which in this case is an unpredictable form, and decide if, and how, the past participle will be marked for agreement with the subject. …

… no student alone possesses the ability to construct the French past compound tense of the reflexive verb 'to remember'. Each student appears to control only a specific aspect of the desired construction. Speaker 1, for example, produces the correct past participle (A1) but the incorrect auxiliary verb. Speaker 2 recognizes the verb as reflexive (A5) but fails to select the appropriate auxiliary *être*. Speaker 3, on the other hand, understands the choice of the auxiliary for reflexive compound past tense forms but does not include the correct reflexive pronoun into his version of the utterance (A7). At this point in the interaction Speakers 1 and 2 synthesize the prior knowledge that has been externalized during the interaction and simultaneously arrive at the correct construction (A9–A12).

The interesting point here is that these three learners are able to construct collectively a scaffold for each other's performance.

▷ *Donato shows how a particular utterance can be socially constructed. What else is needed to show that this results in L2 acquisition?*

▷ *Donato's protocol illustrates the 'negotiation of form' rather than the 'negotiation of meaning'. If he is right and such inter-*

actions can contribute to acquisition what changes need to be made to the input and interaction hypotheses?

▷ *How does Donato's notion of 'scaffolding' differ from Swain's output hypothesis?*

Chapter 6
Psycholinguistic aspects of interlanguage

Text 14
ERIC KELLERMAN: 'Now you see it, now you don't' in
S. Gass and L. Selinker (eds.): *Language Transfer in Language Learning.* Newbury House 1983, pages 113–4

Kellerman considers two constraints on language transfer. The first he refers to as the 'perception of language distance' or the learner's 'psychotypology'. The second constraint concerns the learner's perceptions of the markedness of an L1 structure.

I want now to examine one factor that will act as a *constrainer* or a *trigger* of transfer. This is the learner's notion of the relations between the L1 and L2. [I have suggested] that general typological closeness of L1 to L2 would be capitalized on by learners as a result of a relatively immediate opportunity to identify cognate forms and structures across the two languages. As a natural by-product of this opportunity to make these associations, one would anticipate both facilitation and interference. However, certain interference errors would be resistant to eradication, particularly in environments of minimal linguistic difference. ... Conversely, if L1 and L2 were very different, the lack of available correspondences would, in the initial stages at least, act as a bar to transfer, since the learner is unable to make the necessary cross-lingual tie-ups.

▷ *What languages do you consider 'typologically close' and 'typologically distant' to your own language?*

▷ *Can you think of any forms or structures in your L1 that you would anticipate could be cognate with the forms and structures in a typologically close language?*

Earlier I suggested that any occurrence of linguistic equivalence between L1 and L2, which thus provides the potential for transfer between L1 and L2, will nevertheless not guarantee that facilitation will take place, since L1-induced constraints may act to limit theoretically possible IL forms to an attested subset. The exact nature of what does constitute this subset will, as I have already indicated, depend not only on what I have called the learner's psychotypology but also on a second constraining factor, the *transferability* of the L1 structure, that is, the probability with which this structure will be transferred relative to other structures in the L1. Transferability is to be seen as a theoretical notion, which derives from native speakers' own perception of the structure of their language. If a feature is perceived as infrequent, irregular, semantically or structurally opaque, or in any other way exceptional, what we could in other words call 'psycholinguistically marked', then its transferability will be inversely proportional to its degree of markedness. ... It is important to emphasize that the relative transferability of structures is determined by the L1 and is thus independent of the nature of the L2, though they [*sic*] will interact with the learner's perception of the L1–L2 distance.

▷ *Can you identify structures in your L1 which you perceive to be 'unmarked' and thus potentially transferable?*

▷ *What about structures in your L1 that you perceive as 'marked'?*

▷ *How might the two constraining factors Kellerman considers (i.e. (1) the learner's perception of the L1–L2 distance and (2) the relative transferability of structures) interact?*

Text 15

RICHARD SCHMIDT: 'The role of consciousness in second language learning' in *Applied Linguistics* 11, 1990, pages 129-30

Krashen views 'acquisition' (as opposed to 'learning') as a subconscious process. This text discusses different positions relating to the role of consciousness in L2 acquisition.

One of the more controversial issues in applied linguistics concerns the role of conscious and unconscious processes in second language learning. On the one hand, there are many who believe that conscious understanding of the target language system is necessary if learners are to produce correct forms and use them appropriately. In this view, errors are the result of not knowing the rules of the target language, forgetting them, or not paying attention. There is little theoretical support for the most traditional form of this view; no current theory posits the conscious study of grammar as either a necessary or sufficient condition for language learning. ...

Others firmly believe that language learning is essentially unconscious. Seliger has claimed that 'obviously, it is at the unconscious level that language learning takes place' (Seliger 1983: 187). Krashen (1981, 1983, 1985) has elaborated a theory that rests on a distinction between two independent processes, genuine learning, called 'acquisition', which is subconscious, and conscious 'learning', which is of little use in actual language production and comprehension. ...

A third commonly held position is that the issue of consciousness should be avoided altogether in a theory of language acquisition. McLaughlin, Rossman and McLeod (1983) argue against Krashen's 'learning-acquisition' distinction because it rests on what they consider to be the unsupportable distinction between conscious and unconscious knowledge. In a recent discussion of explicit and implicit knowledge, Odlin recommends divorcing these concepts from the 'notoriously slippery notion of "consciousness" ' (Odlin 1986: 138).

▷ *Schmidt outlines three positions regarding the role of consciousness in L2 acquisition. Which position is compatible with a Vygotskian theory of L2 acquisition? Which position do you think Swain adopts?*

▷ *Which one do you favour? Why?*

Text 16

CLAUS FÆRCH and GABRIELE KASPER: 'Plans and strategies in foreign language communication' in C. Færch and G. Kasper (eds.): *Strategies in Interlanguage Communication*. Longman 1983, pages 36–7

This text considers how to classify communication strategies.

A first broad categorization of communication strategies can be made on the basis of two fundamentally different ways in which learners might behave when faced with problems in communication. Learners can either solve such problems by adopting *avoidance behaviour*, trying to do away with the problem, normally by changing the communicative goal, or by relying on *achievement behaviour*, attempting to tackle the problem directly by developing an alternative plan. On the basis of these two different approaches to problem-solving, we can draw a distinction between two major types of strategies: *reduction strategies*, governed by avoidance behaviour, and *achievement strategies* governed by achievement behaviour.

▷ *Can you think of examples of reduction and achievement communication strategies?*

▷ *One of the achievement strategies Færch and Kasper mention is 'transfer'. What is the difference between 'transfer' as a communication strategy and as a learning process? How might these two types of transfer be distinguished?*

▷ *Færch and Kasper suggest that only achievement strategies are likely to promote L2 acquisition. What do you think their reasoning is? Do you agree?*

Chapter 7
Linguistic aspects of interlanguage

Text 17
MICHAEL LONG: 'Maturational constraints on language development' in *Studies in Second Language Acquisition* 12, 1990, pages 273–4

It has been suggested that there are critical periods that govern when learners are able to achieve native-speaker competence in an L2. This text considers the duration of these critical periods for different aspects of language.

Contrary to recent assertions in the literature, there is growing evidence that maturational constraints are at work in SL learning, and that they are not confined to phonology. Studies showing an initial rate advantage for adults over children and for older over younger children in early syntax and morphology should be interpreted as just that—a short-lived rate advantage. They do not show that older children or adults are better learners. On the contrary, starting after age 6 appears to make it impossible for many learners (and after age 12 for the remainder) to achieve native-like competence in phonology; starting later than the early teens, more precisely after age 15, seems to create the same problems in morphology and syntax. Preliminary results suggest that similar generalizations will eventually be found to hold for lexis and collocation, and for certain discourse and pragmatic abilities.

While the superior long-term achievement of younger learners is consistent with the notion of maturational constraints on most dimensions of SLA, the apparent inability of older learners to attain native-like proficiency if they begin after a certain age further suggests that there is a sensitive period for learning. The precise limits of this period are still unclear. The available data suggest, however, that exposure needs to occur before age 6 to guarantee that an SL phonology can become native-like (given sufficient opportunity) before age 15 if the morphology and syntax are to be native-like, and somewhere between those ages for the remaining linguistic domains. That is to say, there is probably not just one sensitive period for SLA, but several: one for phonology, one for morpho-syntax, and so on. No doubt, as with sensitive periods in many aspects of human and other animal development, there is some overlap due to the relationships among sub-systems across linguistic domains, and some variation across individuals.

The easiest way to falsify such claims would be to produce learners who have demonstrably attained native-like proficiency despite having begun exposure well after the closure of the hypothesized sensitive periods.

▷ *Why do you think older children and adults enjoy 'a short-lived advantage' over children in learning an L2?*

▷ *What explanations can you offer for the failure of adults to achieve native-like competence in an L2?*

▷ *What explanation can you give for the existence of different sensitive periods for phonology and morpho-syntax?*

▷ *Do you know any L2 learners who began learning as adults but have achieved native-like proficiency?*

Text 18

LYDIA WHITE: 'Second language acquisition and universal grammar' in *Studies in Second Language Acquisition* 12, 1990, pages 127–8

In this text White considers how researchers can set about investigating whether Universal Grammar (UG) is still available in L2 acquisition.

It is not sufficient to point to general differences between L1 and L2 acquisition to argue for non-availability of UG, or to general similarities to argue for its availability. UG is a claim about knowledge in a particular domain, a claim that our knowledge of language is constrained by certain abstract but crucial principles. Therefore, the potential availability of UG in L2 acquisition must be investigated within this same domain. If UG is no longer available to adults, and second language acquisition proceeds by means of general cognitive abilities, L2 learners should not be able to work out abstract properties of the L2 which are underdetermined by the input data. Where the input is insufficiently precise to allow L2 learners to induce the relevant properties of the grammar, they should not be able to achieve full success. Thus, one form of evidence for the hypothesis that UG operates in L2 acquisition will be evidence that L2 learners in fact attain the kind of complex and subtle knowledge which is attributable to UG.

However, L1 knowledge is a confounding factor. If a particular principle of UG operates in both the L1 and L2, and if L2 learners show evidence of observing this principle, this could be attributed to transfer of L1 knowledge. Similarly, if L2 learners show evidence of applying L1 parameter settings to the L2, this is actually neutral concerning the availability or non-availability of UG. Thus, the strongest arguments in favor of the operation of UG (complete or partial) in L2 acquisition will be made in cases where effects of the L1 can be minimized.

In order to eliminate the L1 as a source of UG-like knowledge, two situations can be isolated, one relevant to the operation of principles and the other relevant to parameters. In the case of principles, if UG is not available, then L2 learners should *not* be able to sort out aspects of the L2 where both of the following hold:

a some principle operates in the L2 but not the L1, and
b the input underdetermines the L2 grammar.

Similarly, in the case of parameters, L2 learners should not be able to acquire the L2 value of a parameter where:

a the L1 and L2 have different values for some parameter, and
b the input underdetermines the L2 grammar.

If L2 learners successfully arrive at the relevant properties of the L2 under such conditions, then there is support for the claim that UG is still truly accessible, rather than inaccessible or weakly accessible only via the L1.

▷ *What do you think White means by 'general differences between L1 and L2 acquisition'? Can you give examples? Why are these not sufficient to demonstrate the non-existence of UG in L2 acquisition?*

▷ *In what way is the L1 'a confounding factor' in investigating the availability of UG in L2 acquisition? What is White's solution to this problem?*

▷ *What does White mean by 'the input underdetermines the L2 grammar'? Why is it necessary to investigate grammatical properties where this is the case?*

Chapter 8
Individual differences in L2 acquisition

Text 19
PETER SKEHAN: *Individual Differences in Second-language Learning.* Edward Arnold 1989, page 37

Skehan argues that different types of language aptitude may be involved in different types of language processing.

The major point is to connect this aptitude research with contemporary linguistics. Although most linguists aim at the parsimonious and elegant description of language structure, this view has recently come under some attack. In terms of *acquisition*, Peters (1983) proposes that the units of the linguist need not be, and are not likely to be, the units of the language learner. Learners, she proposes, frequently operate with chunks of language on an 'analyse only if you have to' principle. These chunks could potentially (in linguistic terms) be related to one another and therefore stored and produced more economically, but a language user (or learner) will not necessarily carry out such analyses if (a) the separate chunks function effectively in conveying the meanings intended, and (b) the learner is equipped with a memory system which can tolerate this inefficiency and redundancy. ...

The aptitude research seems to embrace both the linguistic and the 'chunking' viewpoints, however, suggesting two different *orientations* to language development—one linguistic, and one memory-based. One type of learner seems to have a language learning orientation which stresses the analysability of language while the other, perhaps more expression-oriented, is more apt to rely on chunks of language and efficient memory. ... What the aptitude research may have been reflecting is the existence of two contrasting orientations to language and language learning.

▷ *What exactly are the 'two contrasting orientations to language and language learning' that Skehan has in mind?*

▷ *Look back at the description of the components of language aptitude in the Survey (page 74). Can you relate the components to the two orientations Skehan refers to?*

▷ *What is your own orientation to language learning?*

Text 20
GRAHAM CROOKES and RICHARD SCHMIDT: 'Motivation: Reopening the research agenda' in *Language Learning* 41, 1991, page 480

In this text, the case for what is referred to as 'intrinsic motivation' (see page 76 in the Survey) is put, particularly where language teaching is involved.

We have referred to the invalidity of SL treatments of motivation in terms of their distance from everyday, nontechnical concepts of what it means to be motivated. When teachers say that a student is motivated, they are not usually concerning themselves with the student's reasons for studying, but are observing that the student does study, or at least engage in teacher-desired behavior in the classroom and possibly outside it. Most teachers wish to motivate students ... and attempt to do so in a variety of ways, of which altering attitudes to the subject matter is just one. In general, it is probably fair to say that teachers would describe a student as motivated if he or she becomes productively engaged in learning tasks, and sustains that engagement, without the need for continual encouragement or direction. They are more concerned with motivation than affect. This teacher-validated use of the term motivation has not been adopted by SL investigators, but it is very close to the concept of motivation that has been substantially explored outside SLA, particularly in social and educational psychology.

▷ *Crookes and Schmidt are reacting to the socio-psychological view of motivation prevalent in second language research. What is this view? (see Survey pages 75–6).*

▷ *What alternative view of motivation do Crookes and Schmidt offer?*

▷ *Can you suggest some of the ways in which teachers attempt to motivate their students other than 'altering attitudes to the subject'?*

Text 21

REBECCA OXFORD: *Language Learning Strategies: What Every Teacher Should Know.* Newbury House 1990, pages 8–9

Learners employ learning strategies to assist them in their attempts to learn an L2. This text identifies different types of learning strategies.

All appropriate language learning strategies are oriented toward the broad goal of communicative competence. Development of communicative competence requires realistic interaction among learners using meaningful, contextualized language. Learning strategies help learners participate actively in such authentic communication. Such strategies operate in both general and specific ways to encourage the development of communicative competence.

It is easy to see how language learning strategies stimulate the growth of communicative competence *in general*. For instance, metacognitive ('beyond the cognitive') strategies help learners to regulate their own cognition and to focus, plan, and evaluate their progress as they move toward communicative competence. Affective strategies develop the self-confidence and perseverance needed for learners to involve themselves actively in language learning, a requirement for attaining communicative competence. Social strategies provide increased interaction and more empathetic understanding, two qualities necessary to reach communicative competence. Certain cognitive strategies, such as analyzing, and particular memory strategies, like the keyword technique, are highly useful for understanding and recalling new information—important functions in the process of becoming competent in using the new language. Compensation strategies aid learners in overcoming knowledge gaps and continuing to communicate authentically; thus, these strategies help communicative competence to blossom.

▷ *What are the different kinds of learning strategies Oxford mentions? Try to write a clear definition of each type and to give an example of each.*

▷ *Think about how you would perform a real-life task in a foreign language (for example, complaining about your room to the manager of a hotel). What specific learning strategies might you use in this task? Try to classify them according to Oxford's general types.*

Chapter 9
Instruction and L2 acquisition

Text 22
PATSY LIGHTBOWN: 'Getting quality input in the second/foreign language classroom' in C. Kramsch and S. McConnell-Ginet (eds.): *Text and Context: Cross-*

Disciplinary Perspectives on Language Study. D.C. Heath
and Company 1991, pages 192–3

*In this extract, Lightbown describes two experimental stud-
ies involving form-focused instruction which she carried out
with Lydia White, Nina Spada, and Leila Ranta.*

In two experimental studies, we provided teachers in the intensive ESL classes (in Quebec) with teaching materials focusing
on two aspects of English that the learners were far from mas-
tering. The aim of these studies was to explore the effect of
introducing more correct examples of target language structures
together with some focused instruction and corrective feedback
so that learners could see how their interlanguage differed from
target language rules.

In the first, we asked some intensive program teachers to
teach students that, even though adverb placement in English is
relatively free, there is one position where English does not normally allow adverbs in simple sentences: between the verb and
direct object. Note that this is not the case in French, where this
position is allowed.

* Mary buys often flowers for her mother.
Marie achète souvent des fleurs pour sa mère.

After two weeks (approximately nine hours of instruction), of
relatively brief daily activities involving both 'consciousness
raising' (through the presentation of examples, corrective feedback on error) and communicative activities where adverbs were
used, students in the experimental group were dramatically better than a control group who had not had these lessons. ... Five
weeks later they were still performing with a high level of accuracy. One year later, however, they had slipped back to a level
not significantly different from the pretest performance. ...

In the second experimental study we prepared instructional
packages for the teachers on the formation of English questions,
both *yes/no* and *wh* types. French has a large variety of ways
to form grammatical questions. French-speaking learners of
English might be expected to assume, once they identify some
of the English question forms that both French and English
permit, that English has the same range of questions (with the
same pragmatic force) as French.

The design of the study was similar to that of the adverb study reported above. The instruction included consciousness raising and communicative activities with opportunities for teachers to provide corrective feedback. And the results of the study were somewhat similar. That is, students performed significantly better after instruction than before instruction on a variety of tasks—oral and written—in which they either produced questions or indicated which of two questions was more correct (or whether both were equally correct or incorrect). The difference was that, six months later, the students were still improving. Their accuracy in using questions and in judging the grammaticality of questions had not slipped back to pre-instruction levels.

▷ *What do the two experiments that Lightbown describes show about the effectiveness of instruction?*

▷ *Why do you think the effects of instruction wore off in the case of adverb position?*

▷ *Why do you think the effects of instruction proved durable in the case of question formation?*

▷ *How could you test your ideas?*

Text 23

FRED ECKMAN, LAWRENCE BELL, and DIANE NELSON: 'On the generalization of relative clause instruction in the acquisition of English as a second language' in *Applied Linguistics* 9, 1988, pages 3 and 8–10

Here is an account of a study that investigated whether L2 learners can generalize knowledge about marked grammatical structures to linked unmarked structures (see page 83 of the Survey).

This paper reports an experimental study intended to test the generalization of instruction in second language learning. A group of students in an English as a second language program served as subjects for special instruction in relative clause formation. The subjects were given a pre-test on combining two sentences into one sentence containing a relative clause where either the subject, object, or object of preposition was the relativized noun phrase. Based on the pre-test results, four equal groups were formed, three of which served as experimental groups and one as the control group. Each experimental group was given instruction on the formation of only one type of relative clause. The subjects were then given a post-test. ...

Each of the pre- and post-tests was scored on the basis of whether or not the student produced the correct target sentence. Only errors relevant to the formation of the target relative clause were counted. ...

... the majority of errors involved the structure of the relative clause itself. A frequent error type was the insertion of a resumptive pronoun in the position from which the NP was relativized. Another error type involved the failure to delete the relativized NP from its original, pre-relativized position. These errors are shown in (a) and (b) respectively:

a   Target: Joan read the book that Martin sold to Bill.
   Error: Joan read the book that Martin sold it to Bill.

b   Target: The teacher found the paper that Alex threw in the trash can.
   Error: The teacher found the paper that Alex threw the paper in the trash can.

... The number of errors per group, broken down by relative clause structure, for both the pre- and post-test are shown in the Table.

Pre-test				Post-test		
	Subj. str.	Obj. str.	OP str.	Subj. str.	Obj. str.	OP str.
Subject group	34	36	42	4	25	38
Object Group	32	32	42	10	12	38
Direct object group	35	39	42	0	4	1
Control group	27	30	42	23	30	42

TABLE 10: *Number of errors per group by relative clause structure*

- ▷ *What do Eckman et al. mean by 'generalization of instruction'?*

- ▷ *Why are relative clauses an appropriate grammatical structure to test whether 'generalization of instruction' takes place?*

- ▷ *What do the results shown in the Table show about the effects of the instruction?*

- ▷ *What are the implications of this study for teaching?*

- ▷ *Do you find this study convincing or do you have some reservations?*

Chapter 10
Conclusion: multiple perspectives in SLA

Text 24

KEVIN GREGG: 'Second language acquisition theory: a case for a generative perspective' in S. Gass and J. Schachter (eds.): *Linguistic Perspectives on Second Language Acquisition.* Cambridge University Press 1989, pages 31 and 35

There is a debate in SLA about the role of theory. Should SLA strive for a single theory that can guide a program of research? Or should it accept a proliferation of theories? Here is one view.

Actually, in the absence of a formal theory, we get not only informal description, but also a proliferation of terminology, either produced ad hoc ('creative construction', Krashen's 'output filter', Tarone's 'capability continuum', the various 'competences', etc.; my favorite invention is 'semantic clout') or imported unthinkingly from other disciplines; added to this are a lot of flow charts and diagrams. In the absence of a theory we run the risk of getting mired in sterile taxonomies that, however plausible or locally useful, are not constrained by any principle. ...

... Although there is a great deal of SLA research going on, what is much harder to find is a research *program*. In SLA research in general, there has been little sense of an overall guiding purpose beyond the general one of finding out things.

▷ *Why do you think terminology proliferated in SLA? Do you think Gregg is right to criticize this?*

▷ *What does Gregg mean by 'a research program'? Do you think he is right to complain that this has been missing from SLA?*

▷ *Of the various perspectives on SLA you have examined in this book (sociolinguistic, discourse, psycholinguistic, linguistic, individual differences, pedagogic) which one do think is best equipped to provide SLA with 'an overall guiding purpose'?*

SECTION 3
References

The references which follow can be classified into introductory level (marked ■□□), more advanced and consequently more technical (marked ■■□), and specialized, very demanding (marked ■■■).

Chapter 1
Introduction: describing and explaining L2 acquisition

■□□

VIVIAN COOK: *Second Language Learning and Language Teaching*. Edward Arnold 1991

A clear account of the main areas of L2 acquisition of relevance to teachers. A useful feature is the use of summary boxes.

■□□

ROD ELLIS: *Understanding Second Language Acquisition*. Oxford University Press 1985

This book constitutes a general introduction to the key issues in SLA and reviews research carried out in the 1970s and early 1980s.

■■□

ROD ELLIS: *The Study of Second Language Acquisition*. Oxford University Press 1994

This provides an up-to-date and very detailed account of SLA. Its length (over 800 pages) makes it best suited for use as a reference book. Features of this book are tables that review research studies in particular areas of enquiry and an extensive glossary.

■□□

SUSAN GASS and LARRY SELINKER: *Second Language Acquisition: An Introductory Course*. Lawrence Erlbaum 1994

This provides a review of the major areas and attempts to integrate these into a single framework. There is a separate chapter on the L2 acquisition of vocabulary. The book also provides 'Points for Discussion', offers L2 data for analysis, and includes a glossary.

■■□

DIANE LARSEN-FREEMAN and MICHAEL LONG: *An Introduction to Second Language Acquisition Research*. Longman 1991

In addition to reviewing the major issues in SLA, this book also provides two excellent chapters on research methodology in SLA. Each chapter is also followed by comprehension and application questions.

■□□

PATSY LIGHTBOWN and NINA SPADA: *How Languages are Learned*. Oxford University Press 1993

A very readable introduction to those issues in SLA which are of direct interest to teachers.

■■□

BARRY MCLAUGHLIN: *Theories of Second-Language Learning*. Edward Arnold 1987

This differs from the other introductory books in that it focuses on the major theories in SLA. These are explained clearly and critiqued fairly.

■■□

BERNARD SPOLSKY: *Conditions for Second Language Learning*. Oxford University Press 1989

Spolsky offers a general theory of L2 acquisition in the form of a series of conditions which are either necessary for or facilitative of L2 acquisition.

■■□

RICHARD TOWELL and ROGER HAWKINS: *Approaches to Second Language Acquisition*. Multilingual Matters 1994

A well-written introduction that focuses on two principal aspects of SLA (UG and variability). Its uniqueness lies in the attempt to develop a general model that incorporates both of these aspects.

Chapter 2
The nature of learner language

■■□

KATHLEEN BARDOVI-HARLIG and DUDLEY REYNOLDS: 'The role of lexical aspect in the acquisition of tense and aspect' in *TESOL Quarterly* 29, 1995, pages 107–31

An interesting account of how various factors shape the development of past tense markers based on the authors' own research. This article informed the discussion of the acquisition of the past tense in the Survey.

■□□

S. PIT CORDER: 'The significance of learners' errors' in *International Review of Applied Linguistics* 5, 1967, pages 161–9

In this seminal article, Corder lays out the rationale for investigating learners' errors.

■□□

S. PIT CORDER: 'Error analysis' in S. Pit Corder and P. Allen (eds.): *The Edinburgh Course in Applied Linguistics*, Vol. 3. Oxford University Press 1974

This provides a clear but technical account of the main procedures involved in identifying, describing, and explaining errors.

■□□

HEIDI DULAY, MARINA BURT, and STEPHEN KRASHEN: *Languge Two*. Oxford University Press 1982

Overall, this book presents a rather partial view of L2 acquisition but the chapter on errors (Chapter 7) is balanced and informative. This book also provides a summary of the early research on accuracy orders.

■□□

JACK RICHARDS: *Error Analysis*. Longman 1974

This contains a number of key articles including Corder's 'The Significance of Learners' Errors' and Selinker's 'Interlanguage'. A minor classic in the field.

■■□

ELAINE TARONE: *Variation in Interlanguage*.
Edward Arnold 1988

This provides a survey of the work on variability in learner language and also examines different theoretical accounts of variability.

■■■

RICHARD TOWELL, ROGER HAWKINS, and NIVES BAZERGUI: 'Systematic and nonsystematic variability in advanced language learning' in *Studies in Second Language Acquisition* 15, 1993, pages 439–60

Very technical, but important because it attempts to show how the stages of L2 acquisition reflect different types of variability.

■□□

GORDON WELLS: *The Meaning Makers*.
Hodder and Stoughton 1986

Wells provides a very readable introduction to the study of L1 acquisition based on his own extensive research. Chapters 2 and 3 deal with acquisitional sequences.

Chapter 3
Interlanguage

There are general accounts of interlanguage theory in Ellis (1994), Gass and Selinker (1994), and Larsen-Freeman and Long (1991)—see references for Chapter 1. A number of early articles on interlanguage can be found in Richards (1974)—see references for Chapter 2.

■■□

S. PIT CORDER: *Error Analysis and Interlanguage*.
Oxford University Press 1981

An invaluable collection of Corder's papers which show something of the development of 'interlanguage' as a theory.

■■■

ALAN DAVIES, CLIVE CRIPER, and ANTHONY HOWATT (eds.): *Interlanguage*. Edinburgh University Press 1984

A set of 'state-of-the-art' papers originally given at a conference in honour of Pit Corder. They reflect the way interlanguage theory developed in the ten or so years from its birth.

■■■

LARRY SELINKER: 'Interlanguage' in *International Review of Applied Linguistics* 10, 1972, pages 209–31

This article is not easy to read, but it gave SLA the term 'interlanguage' and it contains a rich seam of theoretical ideas that is still being mined today.

Chapter 4
Social aspects of interlanguage

■■■

LESLIE BEEBE and HOWARD GILES: 'Accommodation theory: a discussion in terms of second language acquisition' in *International Journal of the Sociology of Language* 46, 1984, pages 5–32

This article critiques the view of variability as a stylistic continuum, outlines Giles's accommodation theory, and applies it to L2 acquisition.

■■□

L. DICKERSON: 'The learner's interlanguage as a system of variable rules' in *TESOL Quarterly* 9, 1975, pages 401–7

An interesting report of an empirical study of Japanese learners' variable use of /z/ in English that illustrates the 'stylistic continuum'.

■■□

BONNY PEIRCE: 'Social identity, investment, and language learning' in *TESOL Quarterly* 29, 1995, pages 9–31

A powerfully argued paper in which the case for a socially constructivist view of L2 acquisition is developed and illustrated through case studies of adult learners.

■■□

JOHN SCHUMANN: *The Pidginization Process: A Model for Second Language Acquisition*. Newbury House 1978

An account of a fossilized learner of English together with an outline of the acculturation model.

■■■

ELAINE TARONE: 'On the variability of interlanguage systems' in *Applied Linguistics* 4, 1983, pages 143–63

Tarone argues the case for viewing the learner's interlanguage as a continuum of styles ranging from the 'careful' to the 'vernacular'.

Chapter 5
Discourse aspects of interlanguage

■■□

R. DONATO: 'Collective scaffolding in L2 learning' in J. Lantolf and G. Appel (eds.): *Vygotskian Approaches to Second Language Research*. Ablex 1994

An well-illustrated account of how learners can co-construct grammatical structures and subsequently use them unassisted.

■■□

EVELYN HATCH (ed.): *Second Language Acquisition*. Newbury House 1978

This collection contains Wagner-Gough's article on scaffolding in learner discourse and Hatch's own seminal article on how discourse shapes L2 acquisition in children and adults.

■■□

EVELYN HATCH: 'Simplified input and second language acquisition' in R. Andersen (ed.): *Pidginization and Creolization as Language Acquisition*. Newbury House 1983

A clear summary of the main types of input modification found in foreigner talk together with a discussion of how they may assist L2 acquisition.

■■□

STEPHEN KRASHEN: *The Input Hypothesis: Issues and Implications*. Laredo Publishing Company 1993

Krashen presents his overall theory of L2 acquisition in which the input hypothesis is central and also reviews relevant research.

■■■

MICHAEL LONG: 'Native speaker/non-native speaker conversation and the negotiation of comprehensible input' in *Applied Linguistics* 4, 1983, pages 126–41

A detailed account of the different types of interactional modification found in the negotiation of meaning Long considers important for L2 acquisition.

■■□

MERRILL SWAIN: 'Three functions of output in second language learning' in G. Cook and B. Seidlhofer (eds.): *Principle and Practice in Applied Linguistics*. Oxford University Press 1995

Swain outlines and illustrates from her own and others' research how output can assist L2 acquisition.

■□□

NESSA WOLFSON: *Perspectives: Sociolinguistics and TESOL*. Newbury House 1983

This provides an account of various aspects of L2 learner discourse, including a summary of her work on compliments.

Chapter 6
Psycholinguistic aspects of interlanguage

L1 transfer

■■■

SUSAN GASS and LARRY SELINKER (eds): *Language Transfer in Language Learning*. Newbury House 1984

This contains a variety of articles on transfer, including those that reflect behaviourist, minimalist, and cognitive positions. Of particular interest is Eric Kellerman's article. A second edition, with some important articles omitted (including Kellerman's) and others added, was published by John Benjamins in 1992.

■■□

TERENCE ODLIN: *Language Transfer.*
Cambridge University Press 1989

An excellent review of the empirical research on language transfer. It examines the evidence for transfer at all language levels—phonology, lexis, grammar, and discourse.

The role of consciousness in L2 acquisition

■■■

NICK ELLIS: *Implicit and Explicit Learning of Languages.*
Academic Press 1994

A collection of papers from the fields of SLA, first language acquisition research, and cognitive psychology reflecting a wide range of views (including Krashen's and Schmidt's) about implicit and explicit learning.

■■■

JAN HULSTIJN and RICHARD SCHMIDT (eds.):
'Consciousness in Second Language Learning' in *AILA Review* 11, 1994

Among other interesting papers, this volume includes Schmidt's attempt to impose some sense and order on the use of the term 'consciousness' in SLA.

■■□

R. SCHMIDT and S. FROTA: 'Developing basic conversational ability in a second language: a case-study of an adult learner' in R. Day (ed.): *Talking to Learn: Conversation in Second Language Acquisition.* Newbury House 1986

A fascinating case study which uses information from Schmidt's diary to make a case for 'noticing' as a conscious and crucial element of L2 acquisition.

Processing operations

■■■

ROGER ANDERSEN: 'The One-to-One Principle of interlanguage construction' in *Language Learning* 34, pages 77–95, 1984

This article describes and illustrates one of the operating principles Andersen believes to be involved in L2 acquisition.

■■■

JURGEN MEISEL, HAROLD CLAHSEN, and MANFRED PIENEMANN: 'On determining developmental stages in natural second language acquisition' in *Studies in Second Language Acquisition* 3, pages 109–35, 1981

This reviews some of the main findings of the ZISA Project on developmental stages in the L2 acquisition of German and outlines the Multidimensional Model.

■■■

THOM HUDSON: 'Nothing does not equal zero: Problems with applying development sequence findings to assessment and pedagogy' in *Studies in Second Language Acquisition* 15, 1993, pages 461–93

Hudson points out some of the problems with the multidimensional model and the research that supports it. Pienemann, Johnston, and Meisel provide a reply in the same volume.

Communication strategies

■■□

ELLEN BIALYSTOK: *Communication Strategies: A Psychological Analysis of Second Language Use.* Blackwell 1990

A review of research into communication strategies together with Bialystok's own theoretical model to account for them.

■■□

CLAUS FÆRCH and GABRIELE KASPER: *Strategies in Interlanguage Communication.* Longman 1983

Still probably the best book overall on communication strategies. It contains the key article by Færch and Kasper on plans and communication strategies.

Chapter 6
Linguistic aspects of interlanguage

■□□

VIVIAN COOK: *Chomsky's Universal Grammar.*
Blackwell 1988

A very clear introduction to Chomsky's theory of language and a helpful chapter on its relationship to L2 acquisition.

■■■

LYNN EUBANK (ed.): *Point Counterpoint: Universal Grammar in the Second Language.* John Benjamins 1991

An interesting collection of papers because it juxtaposes the views of UG believers and non-believers in SLA and thus provides a real debate.

■■■

SUSAN GASS and JACKIE SCHACHTER (eds.): *Linguistic Perspectives on Second Language Acquisition.* Cambridge University Press 1989

A mixture of theoretical articles and reports of empirical studies based on both typological universals and UG.

■■□

THOMAS SCOVEL: *A Time to Speak: A Psycholinguistic Enquiry into the Critical Period for Human Speech.*
Newbury House 1988

A balanced look at a controversial issue and a pleasure to read.

■■□

LYDIA WHITE: *Universal Grammar and Second Language Acquisition.* John Benjamins 1989

Useful for the review of SLA research based on UG.

Chapter 8
Individual differences in L2 acquisition

■■□

GRAHAM CROOKES and RICHARD SCHMIDT: 'Motivation: Reopening the Research Agenda' in Language Learning 31, 1991, pages 469–512

This article challenges Gardner's theory of motivation by arguing the case for viewing it as intrinsic and dynamic.

■■□

K. DILLER (ed.): *Individual Differences and Universals in Language Aptitude*. Newbury House 1981

Contains important articles by Carroll, who reviews his work on language aptitude, and Wesche, who reports a study involving learner-matching.

■■□

R. GARDNER: *Social Pyschology and Second Language Learning: The Role of Attitudes and Motivation*. Edward Arnold 1985

Gardner reviews his years of work on instrumental and integrative motivation.

■■□

J. O'MALLEY and A. CHAMOT: *Learning Strategies in Second Language Acquisition*. Cambridge University Press 1990

A solid survey of the research on learning strategies, including the authors' own research. Good on training learners in the use of strategies.

■□□

REBECCA OXFORD: *Language Learning Strategies: What Every Teacher Should Know*. Newbury House 1990

This classifies, defines, and illustrates a whole host of learning strategies and, as such, is useful as a reference book.

■□□

PETER SKEHAN: *Individual Differences in Second-language Learning*. Edward Arnold 1989

In addition to language aptitude, motivation, and learning strategies, this enjoyable book also reviews research on learning style, anxiety, personality, and learner–instruction matching.

Chapter 9
Instruction and L2 acquisition

■■■

SUSANNE CARROLL and MERRILL SWAIN: 'Explicit and implicit negative feedback: An empirical study of the learning of linguistic generalizations' in *Studies in Second Language Acquisition* 15, 1993, pages 357–86

A report of the authors' research into the effects of negative feedback.

■□□

ROD ELLIS: *Instructed Second Language Acquisition.* Blackwell 1990

An account of how instruction can affect L2 acquisition both directly, through form-focused instruction, and indirectly through classroom interaction.

■■■

BIRGIT HARLEY: 'Functional grammar in French immersion: a classroom experiment' in *Applied Linguistics* 19, pages 331–59, 1989

This article provides an account of Harley's experimental study of form-focused instruction. It also provides an excellent account of a functional approach to teaching grammar.

■■■

KENNETH HYLTENSTAM and MANFRED PIENEMANN (eds.): *Modelling and Assessing Second Language Acquisition.* Multilingual Matters 1985

This book contains a variety of perspectives on the role of form-focused instruction, including Pienemann's ideas about 'teachability' and various responses to it.

■■■

PATSY LIGHTBOWN and NINA SPADA (eds.): 'The Role of Instruction in Second Language Acquisition' (*Studies in Second Language Acquisition* 15, 1993)

A collection of theoretical and research papers dealing with form-focused instruction, including papers by Trahey and White,

Spada and Lightbown, and VanPatten and Cadierno, to which references are made in the Survey.

■■□

J. O'MALLEY: 'The effects of training in the use of learning strategies on acquiring English as a second language' in A. Wenden and J. Rubin (eds.): *Learner Strategies in Language Learning*. Prentice Hall International 1988

An account of three separate experiments in strategy training.

■■■

TERESA PICA: 'Adult acquisition of English as a second language under different conditions of exposure' in *Language Learning* 33, 1983, pages 465–97

A comparison of the acquisition of grammatical morpehemes in tutored, untutored, and mixed groups of learners.

■□□

JACK RICHARDS and TED ROGERS: *Approaches and Methods in Language Teaching*. Cambridge University Press 1986

A clear description of a number of different teaching methods that includes an account of the theories of language learning on which they are based.

Chapter 10
Conclusion: multiple perspectives in SLA

■■■

Applied Linguistics 14/3

This issue is devoted entirely to a discussion of the role of theory in SLA and contains important articles by Gregg, Long, and Schumann, among others.

SECTION 4
Glossary

Page references to Section 1, Survey, are given at the end of each entry.

accessibility hierarchy An implicational ordering of relative pronoun functions (e.g. subject, direct object) in terms of their
degree of **markedness**. [64]

accommodation theory According to this theory, social factors
influence the extent to which speakers seek to make their
speech similar or dissimilar to the speech of their interlocutors.
See **convergence** and **divergence**. [39]

acculturation model According to this theory, various social and
psychological factors govern the extent to which learners are
able to adapt to the target language culture and, thereby,
acquire the L2. See **social distance** and **psychological distance**.
[39]

accuracy order The ranking of grammatical morphemes according to the accuracy with which each morpheme is produced in
learner language. See **acquisition order**. [21]

acquisition order The ranking of grammatical morphemes
according to when each morpheme is acquired by learners.
Some researchers equate the **accuracy order** with the acquisition
order. [21]

auto-input This refers to the possibility that learners' own output can serve as input to their language acquisition mechanisms. [49]

avoidance Avoidance is said to occur when specific target language features are under-represented in learner production in
comparison to native-speaker production. Avoidance may be
caused by **L1 transfer**. [51]

backsliding This is said to occur when learners employ a rule that belongs to an earlier stage of development than the learner's current stage. [34]

behaviourist learning theory A general theory that views all learning as the formation of habits through environmental stimulation. [31]

careful style The term used by Labov to refer to the language used when speakers are attending to and monitoring their speech. *See* **stylistic continuum**. [37]

case study A detailed and usually longitudinal study of a single learner. [6]

communication strategies The strategies used by both native speakers and L2 learners to overcome communication problems resulting from lack of linguistic resources or inability to access them. [51]

comprehensible input That part of the total input that the learner understands and which is hypothesized to be necessary for acquisition to take place. [47]

consciousness-raising A type of form-focused instruction designed to make learners aware of a specific linguistic feature. [85]

contrastive analysis A set of procedures for comparing and contrasting the linguistic systems of two languages in order to identify their structural similarities and differences. [52]

convergence The process by which speakers make their speech similar to their interlocutors' speech. L2 acquisition can be viewed as 'long-term convergence' towards native-speaker norms. *See* **accommodation theory**. [39]

critical period hypothesis This states that target-language competence in an L2 can only be achieved if learning commences before a certain age (e.g. the onset of puberty) is reached. [67]

divergence The process by which speakers make their speech different from their interlocutors' speech. Frequent divergence can be considered to impede L2 acquisition. *See* **accommodation theory**. [39]

errors Deviations in usage which result from gaps in learners' knowledge of the target language: cf. **mistakes**. [12, 17]

explicit knowledge The L2 knowledge of which a learner is aware and can verbalize on request. [56]

foreigner talk The variety of language used by native speakers to address non-native speakers. [45]

form–function mapping The identification by the learner of a particular function which can be performed by means of a particular form. The ensuing 'mapping' may or may not correspond to target-language norms. [28]

formulas Chunks of language that are stored either as complete units (e.g. 'I don't know') or as partially analysed units (e.g. 'Can I have a ____?'). Formulas are lexical in nature: cf. **rule**. [8]

fossilization The processes responsible for the cessation of learning some way short of target-language competence. Most L2 learners' interlanguages fossilize. [29]

free variation The random use of two or more variants of a structure. [28]

global errors Errors that affect overall sentence structure (e.g. word order errors). *See* **local errors**. [20]

implicit knowledge The L2 knowledge of which a learner is unaware and therefore cannot verbalize. [56]

input The samples of oral and written language a learner is exposed to while learning or using a particular L2. [5]

input-based instruction Instruction that aims to teach learners a linguistic item by systematically exposing them to it in the input rather than by giving them opportunities to produce it themselves. [84]

input flooding A type of form-focused instruction that involves supplying learners with plentiful **positive evidence** of a specific linguistic feature. [86]

input hypothesis The hypothesis advanced by Krashen to explain how learners subconsciously acquire language from input they comprehend. *See* **comprehensible input**. [47]

instrumental motivation The degree of effort a learner puts into learning an L2 as a result of the desire to achieve some functional goal (e.g. to pass an exam). [75]

intake That portion of the input that learners attend to and take into short-term memory. Intake may be subsequently incorporated into **interlanguage**. [35]

integrative motivation The degree of effort a learner puts into learning an L2 through an interest in a desire to identify with the target-language culture. [75]

interaction hypothesis The name given to claim that the interactional modifications resulting from the **negotiation of meaning** facilitate acquisition. [47]

interlanguage A term coined by Selinker to refer to the systematic knowledge of an L2 that is independent of both the target language and the learner's L1. [31]

interlanguage continuum The series of interim systems that a learner constructs in the process of acquiring an L2. [33]

investment Learners' commitment to learning an L2, which is viewed as related to the social identities they construct for themselves as learners. [42]

item learning The learning that is involved in learning separate and discrete items of language—e.g. learning that *'maison'* in French takes *'la'* and that *'pantalon'* takes *'le'*: cf. **system learning**. [13]

intrinsic motivation The degree of effort a learner makes to learn an L2 as a result of the interest generated by a particular learning activity. [75]

L1 transfer The process by which the learner's L1 influences the acquisition and use of an L2. [51]

Language Acquisition Device (LAD) According to Chomsky, the innate language faculty responsible for L1 acquisition: cf. **Universal Grammar (UG)**. [32]

language aptitude The special ability that people have, in varying degrees, for learning an L2. [6, 73]

learner language The term given to the language that learners produce in speech and writing during the course of language acquisition. [4]

learning strategy A behavioural or mental procedure used by learners to develop their interlanguages. *See* **communication strategies**. [34, 76]

linguistic context The language that surrounds a particular grammatical feature and which may influence the particular form a learner chooses to use. [26]

local errors Errors that affect single elements in a sentence (e.g. errors in the use of prepositions). *See* **global errors**. [20]

markedness This refers to the general idea that some linguistic features may be more 'basic' or 'natural' than others. More technical definitions based on linguistic theory also exist. [70]

mentalist A mentalist theory of language learning emphasizes the learner's innate capacity for acquiring a language. [13, 31]

mistakes Deviations in usage that reflect learners' inability to use what they actually know of the target language: cf. **errors**. [17]

motivation The effort learners put into learning an L2 as a result of their desire or need to learn it. *See also* **integrative motivation, instrumental motivation, intrinsic motivation**, and **resultative motivation**. [75]

multidimensional model A theory of L2 acquisition proposed by Meisel, Clahsen, and Pienemann. It distinguishes developmental and variational features according to whether they are governed by **processing constraints** or socio-psychological factors. [58]

negative evidence/feedback Information given directly or indirectly to learners that an interlanguage hypothesis is incorrect. [47, 67]

negative transfer Language transfer that results in errors. See **L1 transfer**. [51]

negotiation of meaning The interactive work that takes place between speakers when some misunderstanding occurs. It results in interactional modifications hypothesized to aid acquisition. [46]

noticing The process by which learners pay conscious attention to linguistic features in the input. [55]

notice the gap The process by which learners pay conscious attention to the differences between linguistic features in the input and their own output. [57]

omission Deviations in usage that arise when learners leave out words or parts of words (e.g. omission of the article in 'He went into shop'). [19]

operating principles Slobin's term for the strategies children use during L1 acquisition to segment and analyse input, and which account for regular properties of their output. [57]

overgeneralization The oversuppliance of an interlanguage feature in contexts in which it does not occur in target-language use (e.g. 'He ated ice-cream.') Overgeneralizations result in errors. [19]

overuse The overuse of some feature (e.g. simple coordinate structures) where some other feature (e.g. relative clauses) is preferred in target-language use. Overuse may or may not result in errors. [11, 52]

parallel distributed processing A model of language that views language use and acquisition as involving a complex network of interconnections between units rather than rules. [62]

pidginization The process by which pidgins (i.e. contact languages) are formed; according to Schumann, L2 acquisition may involve a similar process. [40]

positive evidence Input that shows the learner what is grammatical but not what is ungrammatical. [66]

positive transfer Language transfer that facilitates the acquisition of target-language forms. *See* **L1 transfer**. [51]

poverty of the stimulus The inability of input to provide the linguistic information needed for language acquisition. [66]

processing constraints Mechanisms that block learners' ability to perform the permutations involved in different grammatical structures (e.g. produce *wh-* questions with inversion). [59]

production-based instruction A type of form-focused instruction that aims to teach a specific linguistic feature by eliciting sentences containing it from the learner. [84]

psycholinguistic context The aspects of the context in which communication takes place which influence the extent to which learners are able to plan or self-correct what they say or write. [27]

psychological distance The distance between the learner and the target-language community resulting from psychological factors such as language shock and motivation. *See* **accommodation theory**. [40]

restructuring The process by which learners reorganize their interlanguage in the light of new evidence about the target language. It can occur as a result of a shift from **item learning** to **system learning**. [23]

restructuring continuum This refers to the idea that interlanguage development consists of learners gradually replacing L1 rules with target-language rules. [54]

resultative motivation The motivation that learners develop as a result of their success in learning an L2. [75]

rule A mental representation of some abstract property of grammar. Rules are part of grammatical competence and allow a speaker to construct entirely novel sentences: cf. **formulas**. [13, 19]

scaffolding The process by which learners utilize discourse to help them construct structures that lie outside their competence. [48]

sequence of acquisition The stages of development through which learners pass when acquiring grammatical structures such as past tense or learning how to perform language functions such as requests. [21]

silent period Some L2 learners, especially children, undergo a lengthy period during which they do not try to speak, although they may engage in 'private speech'. [20]

situational context The actual situation in which communication takes place. Situational factors such as who a learner is talking to influence the choice of linguistic forms. [26]

social distance The distance between the learner and the target-language community resulting from various social factors such as 'social dominance' and 'enclosure'. *See* **acculturation model**. [40]

speech act An action performed by the use of an utterance, in speech or writing, to communicate. [53]

stylistic continuum The idea that a variable interlanguage consists of a number of styles ranged from a **careful style** to a **vernacular style**. [37]

system learning Learning the abstract rules that underlie the use of linguistic items, e.g. learning when a French noun takes '*la*' and when it takes '*le*'. [13]

target language The language that a learner is trying to learn. [4]

teachability hypothesis The hypothesis that teaching learners a grammatical structure will only be successful if they are developmentally ready to learn it. [82]

transfer *See* **L1 transfer**. [19]

transitional constructions The interim grammatical structures that learners manifest during the **sequence of acquisition**. Different interim structures are evident at different stages of development. [23]

Universal Grammar (UG) Chomsky's term for the abstract principles that comprise a child's innate knowledge of language and that guide L1 acquisition. [65]

U-shaped course of development The pattern of learning evident when learners use a correct target-language form at one stage, replace it with an ungrammatical interlanguage form, and then finally return to use of the correct target-language form. [23]

vernacular style The term used by Labov to refer to the language used when speakers are communicating spontaneously and freely and consequently not attending to the forms they choose. *See* **stylistic continuum**. [38]

zone of proximal development Vygotsky uses this term to refer to the cognitive level that a child is not yet at but is capable of performing at with adult guidance. [48]

Acknowledgements

The author and publisher are grateful to the following for permission to reproduce extracts from copyright material:

Ablex Publishing Corporation for extracts from Richard Donato: 'Collective scaffolding in second language learning' in J. Lantolf and G. Appel (eds.): *Vygotskian Approaches to Second Language Research* (1994).

Addison Wesley Longman Ltd. for an extract from Claus Færch and Gabriele Kasper: 'Plans and strategies in foreign language communication' in Claus Færch and Gabriele Kasper (eds.): *Strategies in Interlanguage Communication* (Longman 1983).

Edward Arnold/Hodder & Stoughton Educational for extracts from Peter Skehan: *Individual Differences in Second Language Learning* (Edward Arnold 1989).

Cambridge University Press for extracts from Kevin Gregg: 'Second language acquisition theory: a case for a generative perspective' in S. Gass and J. Schachter (eds.): *Text and Context: Cross Disciplinary Perspectives on Language Study* (1989); and for extracts from *Studies in Second Language Acquisition* as follows: Rod Ellis: 'Learning to communicate in the classroom: A study of two language learners' requests' (Vol. 14, 1992); Michael Long: 'Maturational constraints on language development' (Vol. 12, 1990); Lydia White: 'Second language acquisition and universal grammar' (Vol. 12, 1990).

A. R. Evans on behalf of Stephen Krashen for an extract from Stephen Krashen: *The Input Hypothesis: Issues and Implications* (Laredo Publishing Company 1993).

Heinle & Heinle for extracts from Richard Schmidt: discussion section of 'Interaction, acculturation, and the acquisition of communicative competence: A case study of an adult' in N. Wolfson and E. Judd (eds.): *Sociolinguistics and Second Language Acquisition* (Newbury House 1983); extracts from Herlinda Cancino, Ellen Rosansky, and John Schumann: 'The acquisition of English negatives and interrogatives by native Spanish speakers' in E. Hatch (ed.): *Second Language Acquisition* (Newbury House 1978); extracts from John Schumann: *The Pidginization Process* (Newbury House 1978); extract from Eric Kellerman: section entitled 'Psychotypological constraints on transfer' of 'Now you see it, now you don't' in S. Gass and L. Selinker (eds.): *Language Transfer in Language Learning* (Newbury House 1983); an extract from R. Oxford: section entitled 'Communicative competence as the main goal' in *Language Learning Strategies: What Every Teacher Should Know* (Newbury House 1990).

Research Club in Language Learning for an extract from Graham Crookes and Richard Schmidt: 'Motivation: Reopening the Research Agenda' in *Language Learning* 41, 1991.

Patsy Lightbown for extracts from Patsy Lightbown: 'Getting quality input in the second/foreign language classroom' in C. Kramsch and S. McConnell-Ginet (eds.): *Text and Context: Cross-disciplinary Perspectives on Language Study* (D. C. Heath and Company 1992).

Oxford University Press for extracts from S. Pit Corder: 'The significance of learners' errors' and from 'Language continua and the interlanguage hypothesis', both in *Error Analysis and Interlanguage* (1980); extracts from Merrill Swain: 'Three functions of output in second language learning' in G. Cook and B. Seidlhofer (eds): *Principle and Practice in Applied Linguistics* (1995); and for extracts from *Applied Linguistics* as follows: Kevin Gregg: 'The variable competence model of second language acquisition, and why it isn't' (Vol. 11, 1990); Elaine Tarone: 'On variation in interlanguage: A response to Gregg' (Vol. 11, 1990); Richard W. Schmidt: introduction to 'The role of consciousness in second language learning' (Vol. 11, 1990); Fred Eckman, Lawrence Bell, and Diane Nelson: 'On the generaliza-

tion of relative clause instruction in the acquisition of English as a
second language' (Vol. 9, 1988).

TESOL, Inc. and the authors for an extract from Michael Long:
'Native speaker/non-native speaker conversation in the second-
language classroom' in M. Clarke and J. Handscombe (eds.): *On
TESOL '82* copyright © 1982 by Teachers of English to
Speakers of Other Languages, Inc.; extracts from Bonny N.
Peirce: 'Social identity, investment, and language learning' in
TESOL Quarterly (Vol. 29, 1995) copyright © 1995 by
Teachers of English to Speakers of Other Languages, Inc.

Despite every effort to trace and contact copyright holders before
publication, this has not always been possible. If notified the publisher will be pleased to rectify any errors or omissions at the
earliest opportunity.